RICHMOND PARK

RICHMOND PARK

The History of a Royal Deer Park

by

Michael Baxter Brown

ROBERT HALE · LONDON

Robert Hale Limited
Clerkenwell House
Clerkenwell Green
London EC1R oHT

British Library Cataloguing in Publication Data
Brown, Michael Baxter
    Richmond Park: the history of a royal deer park.
    1. Richmond Park (London, England) – History
    2. London (England) – Parks – History
    I. Title
    942.1'95   DA685.R5
    ISBN 0-7090-2163-1

Photoset in Great Britain by
Rowland Phototypesetting Ltd, Bury St Edmunds, Suffolk
and printed by St Edmundsbury Press
Bury St Edmunds, Suffolk
Bound by Hunter & Foulis Ltd

Contents

Picture credits

London Transport Executive, 12, 44;
Land Use Consultants, 14–15;
John K. Fawcett, 24, 27, 30 (top), 32, 171 (inset);
Geoffrey Kinns, 30 (bottom), 52–3, 75;
Courtesy of the British Library, 37;
Raymond Gill collection, 43, 85, 122–3, 128–9;
Ron Bell, 50, 116–17;
the Lamport Hall Trust, 56;
London Borough of Richmond upon Thames Reference Service, 68–9,
    79, 94–5, 96;
private collection, 72;
Christina and Bamber Gascoigne, 75, 104, 120–1;
Valerie Warren, FSAL, SGA, 84, 93, 111, 114, 131, 137, 154, 167;
The Richmond Society (History Section), 83;
the Sawyer family, 89, 140;
the Royal Horticultural Society, 90;
by permission of the DOE, 106–7, 152–3, 161, 163;
Mrs C. Pratt (*née* Burwood), 113;
Jane Miller, 124–5, 164, 165, 170–1, 176–7;
Illustrated London News, 151;
Walter Westcott, 157;
Aerofilms, 158–9;
Brian Alderson, 178.

List of Illustrations

Foreword

THATCHED HOUSE LODGE
RICHMOND PARK
SURREY

Our National Heritage, in the form of ancient monuments, great houses, and the arts, is well publicised – and deservedly so. Our gardens, and the work of England's landscape architects from the 18th century onward, are famed throughout the world. But one jewel in the crown of that heritage – the classical English deer park – has not attracted the same attention, despite the fact that a wonderful example lies not ten miles from the heart of London.

Richmond Park is unique. For it is not just a monument in which the historic character of English parkland is preserved; it is an important amenity which serves a vast population well.

This book, I am sure, will promote a deeper understanding and appreciation of what Richmond Park is all about, and by doing so, will play some part in protecting this jewel, with its combined attributes, for the benefit of many generations to come.

Angus Ogilvy.

Acknowledgements

I wish to thank Her Majesty the Queen for her gracious permission to quote from, and refer to, papers in the Royal Archives at Windsor.

To the Hon Angus Ogilvy I express my gratitude for gracing the book with his Foreword.

Invaluable help and advice was received from Miss V. J. Langton, MVO, Registrar of the Royal Archives, Windsor, and Miss E. R. Masters, Deputy Keeper of the Records, Corporation of London, and their respective staffs.

I owe a great deal to Mr and Mrs R. Sawyer, Mr H. Sawyer, and his daughter, Mrs A. Stubbs, for they allowed me access to the Sawyer Family papers, and offered me much kindness and courtesy.

Mr R. Gill led me to the sources which enabled me to expand on the lives of the Carlile family, and provided other useful information.

To the following people who answered enquiries with interest and enthusiasm, or contributed in many other ways, my grateful thanks: The Hon F. David Astor, Professor G. W. S. Barrow, His Grace the Duke of Buccleugh, Professor L. M. C. Cantor, the late Dr D. Chapman, Mrs N. Chapman, Mr J. W. A. Dyer, Mr J. Fawcett, Mr R. G. Flenley, Mrs P. Fletcher-Jones, Dr J. M. Gilbert, Dr P. Hammond, Mr D. Hart-Davis, Mr R. Hase, Mr C. Hibbert, Miss G. Holmes, Miss D. Howard, Mr P. Johnstone, Dr A. McDiarmid, Mr M. Mendoza, CVO, Mr G. Peacock, CVO, Mrs S. Pugh, Julia Turner, Dr J. E. Vipond, Mr K. G. Whitehead, Mr G. M. Wilson.

The staff of the Public Records Office, Kew, and of the British Library I commend for their efficiency and patience; my colleagues at the Department of the Environment I thank for their practical assistance and interest.

Last, but by no means least, I am indebted to my wife Sandra: her services as a typist, her endless patience and her earnest encouragement were major contributions.

Fallow deer in Richmond Park, poster by Sharland, 1911

I

Introduction

Until the end of the Middle Ages, that is towards the close of the fifteenth century, a park (the word is derived from the Old English *pearroc*) was simply an enclosed parcel of land, the purpose of which was to retain the beasts of the chase, which group of animals included deer. The Domesday Survey (1086) records that there were then thirty-five parks in England[1] and that the King, William I (1066–87), had an interest in at least two, Oakley in Buckinghamshire, and Watchingwell in the Isle of Wight.[2] The Survey also describes another type of enclosure, the *haye* or *haiae*, of which there were well over a hundred, most of them concentrated in Cheshire, Shropshire and Herefordshire.[1] Hayes were hedged or paled (fenced) enclosures into which deer were driven and controlled, so that they could more easily be slaughtered with the comparatively primitive weapons of the age. They were mainly associated with roe deer[3] but were also used for the taking of other animals, and as recently as the late eighteenth century hare hayes were being used in Richmond Park.[4]

There is no doubt that hayes were a feature of Saxon England, and it is possible that parks, in some form, also pre-date the Norman Conquest. By the reign of King Canute (1016–35) areas of land had been set aside as royal hunting preserves, and the hunting therein protected by regulation.[5]

'And it is my will that every man have the right to hunt in his own wood and in the fields on his own property, and that every man leave my hunting alone wherever I wish peace to be kept, on pain of full punishment.'[6] Thus reads one of the 'Laws of Cnut'.

Deer, which were the prime quarry of the hunt, have no respect for the boundaries of man, unless the boundaries are a sufficient physical obstacle to prevent egress or ingress. If the freeholder's land was adjacent to a royal hunting preserve, he would have had incentive to restrain his potential quarry within his own property. The development of the haye into an enclosure of sufficient size to allow hunting to take place within its

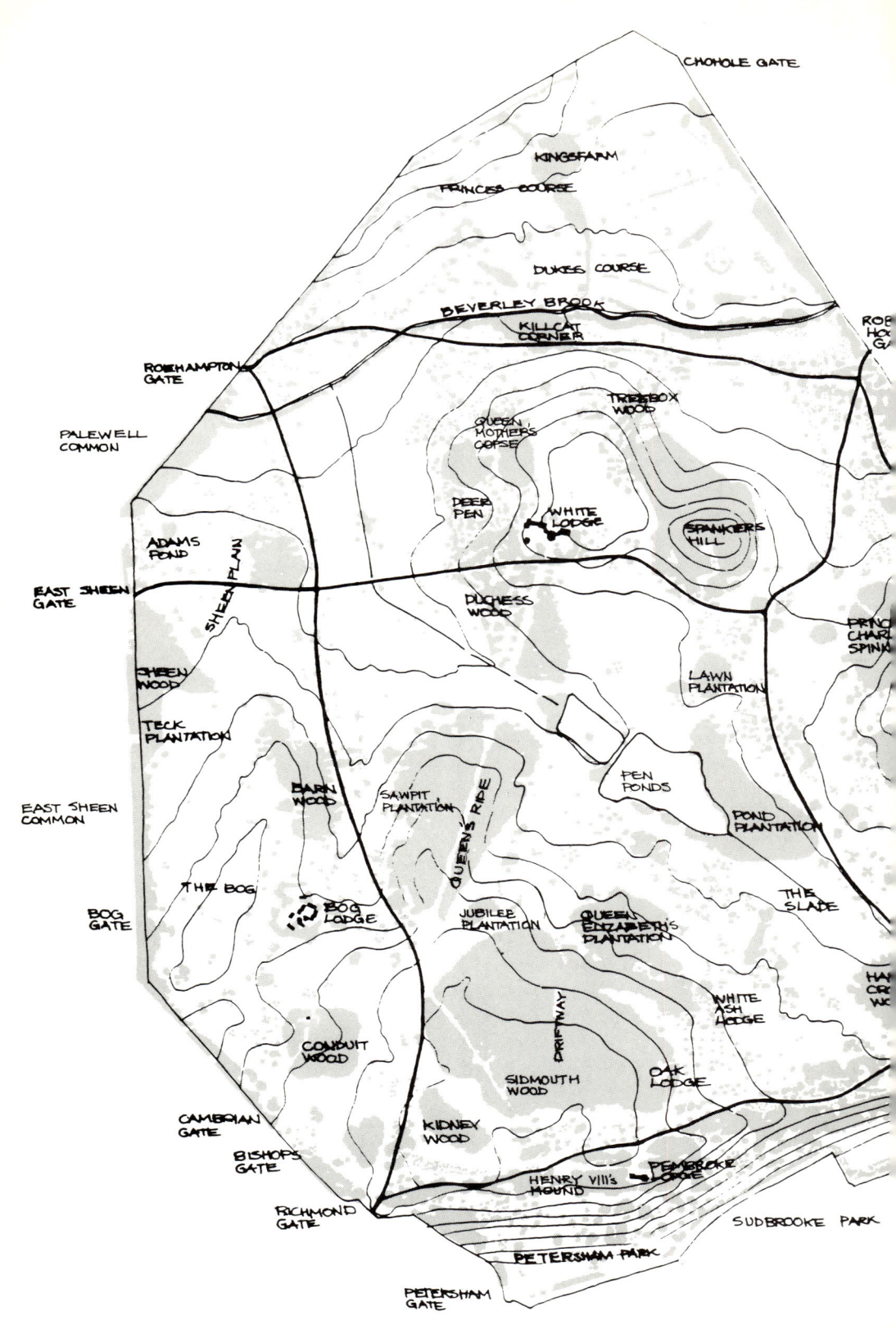

CHOHOLE GATE

KINGSFARM

PRINCESS COURSE

DUKES COURSE

BEVERLEY BROOK

KILLCAT CORNER

ROB HO G

TREEBOX WOOD

QUEEN MOTHER'S COPSE

ROEHAMPTON GATE

PALEWELL COMMON

DEER PEN

WHITE LODGE

SPANKERS HILL

ADAMS POND

SHEEN PLAIN

EAST SHEEN GATE

DUCHESS WOOD

PRINC CHARL SPINN

SHEEN WOOD

LAWN PLANTATION

TECK PLANTATION

EAST SHEEN COMMON

BARN WOOD

SAWPIT PLANTATION

QUEEN'S RIDE

PEN PONDS

POND PLANTATION

THE BOG

BOG LODGE

JUBILEE PLANTATION

QUEEN ELIZABETH'S PLANTATION

THE SLADE

BOG GATE

HA CR W

WHITE ASH LODGE

CONDUIT WOOD

DRIFTWAY

SIDMOUTH WOOD

OAK LODGE

CAMBRIAN GATE

KIDNEY WOOD

BISHOPS GATE

RICHMOND GATE

HENRY VIII's MOUND

PEMBROKE LODGE

SUDBROOKE PARK

PETERSHAM PARK

PETERSHAM GATE

bounds would have been a logical means of achieving this. In this the medieval deer park could conceivably have had its beginnings.

Following the Norman Conquest, the royal hunting preserves of the Saxon era soon developed into the royal forests. Vast tracts of land were proclaimed 'royal forest' by the Norman monarchs, including the whole of the county of Essex. In number and area the royal forests reached their peak during the reign of Henry II (1154–89), after which they steadily diminished, not least as a result of the Magna Carta (1215) and the Charter of the Forest, which followed two years later. A medieval forest consisted not only of woodland but also of great areas of open land, rough pasture and natural water. The Norman kings, obsessed as they were with hunting, introduced a system of regulations, the harsh Forest Laws, designed to protect the royal hunting grounds, the beasts of the chase and, to a lesser degree, the revenues produced in, and by, the forests. The

Plan of Richmond Park, 1983

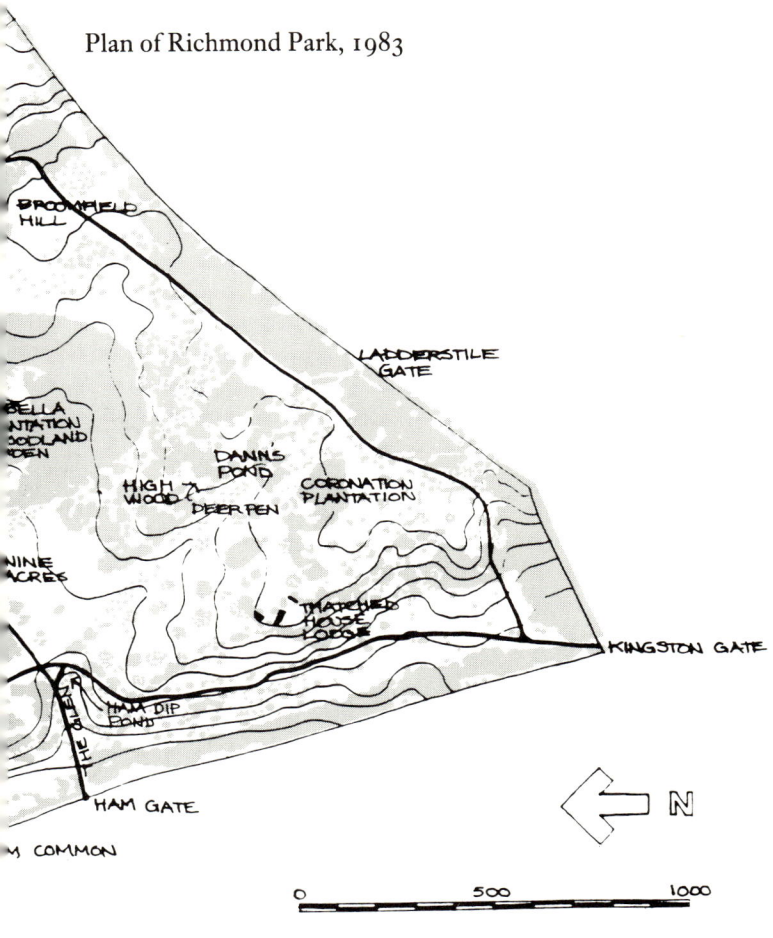

Forest Laws constituted a legal system independent of Common Law, and the word 'forest' was in itself a legal term, defining the huge areas of land protected by this system.

The growth of the medieval deer park coincided with the expansion of the royal forests and the rigorous enforcement of the Forest Laws. They were a device which enabled the nobility, the Church and the wealthy landlord to own their private hunting grounds, stocked with deer, without breaching the Forest Laws. An area of land could not be 'imparked' at will, however, and it was usually necessary to obtain a licence from the king before establishing a park. The licences were a useful source of revenue for the Crown because they could be bought, but they were also granted in return for rendering some important service to the Crown. The grant sometimes included a number of deer from a royal forest to stock the new park. In practice, not all medieval parks were established with proper authority, and in Oxfordshire it seems that only about a quarter were in fact licensed.[7] The number of medieval deer parks in England reached a peak in the mid thirteenth century, at which time there were at least nineteen hundred.[8]

The park provided better opportunity for a successful chase than did the forest, because the quarry was more readily available within its confines. 'Instant' hunting was possible, a useful asset when important entertainment was required. Within the park deer could be more easily managed and controlled. A regular and secure supply of venison was to hand. No doubt those were some of the advantages which prompted a succession of kings from Henry I (1100–1135) to Edward III (1327–77) to create royal parks, in addition to the large number of royal forests already at their disposal. Parks came into the hands of the Crown for other reasons too: for example, as a result of the confiscation of a traitor's estates, or during the minority of an heir, although parks thus acquired were usually 'royal' only for a limited period. Royal parks also figured prominently in royal dowry settlements, and in the later Middle Ages several were granted to religious orders for the establishment of monasteries.

A typical medieval deer park consisted of a mixture of woodland, rough pasture or meadow (grassy glades known as 'launds' or 'lawns') and waste-land, in varying proportion. Their location was commonly some distance away from castle or manor house, probably because outlying lands were not suitable for cultivation. The majority of parks were between forty and eighty acres (fifteen and thirty hectares) in area, but there were a number of much larger parks, some of which belonged to the Crown. The royal park of Woodstock, in Wychwood Forest, Oxfordshire, probably imparked by Henry I at the beginning of the twelfth century, was four hundred hectares.[8] Clarendon, another Royal Park in Clarendon

Forest, Wiltshire, which was imparked between 1225–8,[9] measured three miles across.

The shape was usually roughly circular or elliptical, so that the greatest area of land could be enclosed within the shortest possible perimeter. Occasionally a natural barrier, such as a wide river, provided a section of the boundary, an example being Twickenham Park and the River Thames. First mention of this park, in the manor of Isleworth, Middlesex, is made in 1268, and it had become a royal park by 1300.[10] The reasons for shape, and the occasional use of natural barriers, were economical. Many medieval parks were bounded by massive earthworks, a wide ditch with a high earth embankment behind it, on top of which was erected a paling fence. This was the park pale, expensive to build and expensive to maintain.

Within some parks there were fenced enclosures, particularly in those in which timber and underwood were cropped as a source of revenue. This usually took the form of coppicing, where it was necessary to protect the crop from the depredations of the deer. Few parks could provide sufficient natural food to sustain their deer stocks throughout the year, and it was common practice to augment natural food supplies during the winter. Sometimes hay for this purpose was grown within the park, and it was necessary to enclose the hay fields.

Another feature of the medieval park was the fishpond, or ponds. Fish were an important source of protein in the Middle Ages, and there were often groups of two or three fishponds in a park, usually sited along the length of a natural water course. The arranging of ponds in groups had the advantage of allowing one of the ponds to be cleaned without upsetting the regular supply of fish, and different ponds could be reserved for different species of fish, or for fish of the same age group.[7]

Also associated with many a medieval park was the park lodge. Temporary accommodation for hunting parties was required usually because the park was some distance from the main residence, and in some cases such accommodation may have served, on a more permanent basis, as a residence for the park keeper. Hunting lodges within, or adjacent to, royal parks were frequently used by the monarch. Edward III rebuilt the lodge in Beckley Park, Oxfordshire, which was in royal hands during the fourteenth century, and he reputedly built a new lodge for his own use in Worldham Park, Hampshire, which came into the possession of the Crown in 1374. In some instances the hunting lodges were developed into palatial royal residences, an example being the thirteenth-century palace in Woodstock Park.[9]

The Black Death (1348) marked the beginning of the slow decline of the medieval deer park. Depopulation caused by the plague created labour shortages, and medieval parks, with their massive earthwork boundary pales to maintain, were dependent on the availability of a large pool of labour. Other factors were also involved: during the latter years of the reign of Edward III the Forest Laws were losing much of their impetus, and there were basic changes in farming practice. Although the royal parks were not affected to the same extent as those in private hands, some of the less important were leased for long periods. Others, in whole or in part, were granted to various religious orders, as was Twickenham Park, part of which was granted by Henry V (1413–22) to the Order of St Bridget in 1415.[10]

Although the medieval park was on the wane, a new concept in parks began to emerge in the later Middle Ages, with the emphasis moving away from hunting, towards amenity. The new generation of parks was often directly associated with a major residence and occupied what was once arable or pasture land. Features such as tree-lined avenues were introduced. A certain amount of formality gradually became apparent. Cardinal Wolsey's great parks of Hampton Court and Bushy, associated with the palace which he built beside the Thames, developed from this concept. The palace, gardens and parks were conceived as a whole, contained within the perimeter walls, all three units being intimately associated with one another. The medieval influence was not altogether absent, for the parks were deer parks, designed for hunting. They became royal parks in 1525, when Henry VIII (1509–47) acquired Hampton Court from the Cardinal.

The age of the classical medieval deer park was, however, long past when Clarendon recorded that, 'The King, who was excessively affected to hunting and the sport of the field, had a great desire to make a great park for red as well as fallow deer between Richmond and Hampton Court.'[11] The King was Charles I (1625–49), and the park Richmond Park, known originally as Richmond Great Park or Richmond New Park. It is generally accepted that the park was completed, ready for the King's use, in 1637.

The King's new park was bounded by a brick wall, and not by a pale. He was reluctantly obliged to permit public access from the beginning, albeit only to a limited extent, something which would not even have been considered in the parks of the Middle Ages. But in almost every other respect, as will be explained in the chapters ahead, the park which Charles I created was essentially of the same design as that of a medieval deer park. This in direct contrast to the fashion of amenity parkland, with its element of formality, which was then in vogue.

In the first phase of its existence, the *raison d'être* of the park was that of a deer and game hunting preserve, as Charles I had intended. Deer hunting had come to an end by the mid eighteenth century, but within fifty years a new *raison d'être*, still based on the deer herds, had evolved: that of the provision of large quantities of venison for distribution by royal warrant, a tradition whose roots are buried in the Forest Laws of earlier centuries. Although the tradition still survives, it is now but a token to an ancient custom, and the quantities of venison involved are minimal compared with the huge amounts which the park was obliged to provide for much of the nineteenth century. Today Richmond Park is in its third phase, that of amenity, aesthetic appeal and conservation – not so much the preservation of red and fallow deer, the two species which are found in the park, but the conservation of park deer in a traditional and historic setting in which the basic concepts of the classical medieval deer park are still evident.

The three eras cannot be precisely defined. The last recorded visit of the Royal Buckhounds to the park in 1753[12] could be taken to mark the end of deer hunting; in fact a slender association with deer hunting lingered on until the 1930s. Venison is still distributed by royal warrant. The ornamental value of the park received official recognition as early as 1649, when, out of royal ownership for the only time in its history, it was gifted to the City of London by Cromwell's Parliament. Parliamentary dictates regarding the new owners' responsibilities included that of preserving it as a park 'without Destruction, and to remain as an ornament to the City'.[13] Further official recognition came in 1872 when the Lords Commissioners of HM Treasury acknowledged the aesthetic value of the deer herds: 'Their Lordships considering the great addition which the presence of the herds make to the beauty of the (Royal) Parks are not prepared to direct that they should be removed.'[14]

Over the centuries Richmond Park has proved exceptionally resilient to change. Hardly a square metre has been lost since it was first enclosed. In 1637 the park was surrounded by estates, farms and common land. Today, apart from the buffers of Wimbledon Common and the smaller Ham and Sheen Commons, it stands in the middle of suburbia. In earlier years public use was, in the main, restricted to the relatively small local population. It now caters for a vast population and attracts many overseas visitors. During the past few decades the volume of traffic on the carriageways has increased dramatically; on Thursday 18 October 1973, when the park was open to vehicular traffic for 12½ hours, no fewer than 21,139 vehicles passed through.[15] From time to time, and for varying periods, usually during times of national emergency, substantial areas have been utilized for military and agricultural purposes. The park has successfully withstood those many and varied pressures without yielding up its historic character.

'Richmond Park, the most spacious and in many aspects the most important of the Royal Parks, is a national monument of outstanding character. In no other park is the grand cycle of nature so manifest. It provides for the enjoyment of a vast population some of the most striking of the amenities of our historic parklands.'[16] Thus did the Ministry of

Works Advisory Committee on Forestry (Royal Parks) describe Richmond Park in the introduction of their report to the Minister following an inspection of the trees in 1961.

Richmond Park was created for deer. Their continuing presence has been responsible for its survival in a state which deserves the accolade of 'a national monument'.

2

Fallow, Red and Roe Deer

Deer are ungulates; that is, they belong to that group of plant-eating mammals which, in most cases, have an even number of hooved toes on each foot. They are also ruminants, a term which describes the group of ungulates that chew cud. All ruminants have a specialized digestive system in which the stomach is divided into four compartments. When a ruminant is grazing, the food is taken down directly to the first, and largest, of those compartments, the rumen. Later, when the animal is resting, the undigested food is regurgitated, a little at a time, to be thoroughly chewed before being passed down to the second chamber, the omasum, bypassing the rumen. The cud passes through the remainder of the chambers in turn, where the digestive process is completed with the assistance of a population of specialized micro-organisms.

In the park, grass is the main food of both red and fallow deer. Rushes, sedges and herbs are also grazed. Foxgloves, nettles and thistles are left well alone, nor is bracken eaten, except possibly in the early summer when the fresh tips may be nibbled in limited quantity. The leaves of most deciduous trees, where they can be reached, are browsed, horse chestnut leaves being a particular favourite. Conifers, holly and ivy are palatable and the young shoots of gorse relished. Most shrubs will be eaten if the opportunity presents itself. Brambles, both leaves and fruit, are very acceptable, and even rhododendron will be tried although probably only when other food supplies are scarce. Roses are a great delicacy.

Hence the lack of mid-level vegetation in the open parkland; the absence of a shrub and undergrowth layer betwixt the sward and the bottom of the tree canopy. Only bracken fills the gap, and it dies down in late autumn, leaving nothing until the new fronds appear in May. Mature gorse in the north-west of the park manages to survive, as does the ubiquitous *Rhododendron ponticum* (the common, purple-flowered rhododendron which, although not an indigenous shrub, is established in a more or less natural state throughout the British Isles) in the woods of Spanker's Hill. But both gorse and rhododendron were well established before the two locations were thrown open to the deer.

Deer strip and eat the bark of young trees, particularly during hard winter weather. They also browse on the young shoots and twigs. Continual browsing of leaves, shoots and twigs within reach of deer produces a uniform and even 'browse line', not so noticeable in natural woodland but very clearly defined in a well-stocked deer park. The browse line is indeed a traditional feature of deer parks and in Richmond Park is two metres and more above ground level, this being the height which red deer can reach when reared up on their hind legs. Bark, young shoots, twigs and leaves are an important part of the diet of deer, and in most deer parks young shoots and twigs, as well as bark, are naturally available only in limited quantity. In Richmond Park this is overcome by allowing the deer access to felled trees and fallen branches and limbs for a few days before the 'brash' (leaves, small branches, twigs) is cleared away or burnt.

Fruit, in due season, is another important constituent of the diet. Acorns are much relished. They are usually ignored until ripe, but occasionally a fallow deer will succumb to temptation after a September gale has brought a shower of unripe acorns down, sometimes with fatal results. Chestnuts are also eagerly sought, and it is a comical sight to see a fallow mouthing a chestnut, trying to break open the husk to get to the nut itself.

Fallow deer rarely seem to drink, their moisture intake coming from dew and the water content of vegetation. Red deer, on the other hand, make much more use of water and are frequently to be seen drinking. They swim well, and hinds (mature female red deer) and calves (the young red deer) are often to be found wallowing in water on hot summer days.

The most obvious feature which distinguishes deer from other ruminants is the antlers, which are carried by adult males of most deer species. They are not horns. Horns are generally unbranched, permanent structures borne by both male and female of the horn-bearing ruminants, whereas antlers, often much branched are grown and shed annually. They grow from permanent, bony structures, called 'pedicles', which are an integral part of the frontal bones of the skull. Whilst they are growing, antlers are covered with a soft, furry skin, known as 'velvet', which carries blood and nutrients to the growing tissue. During this stage the antlers are soft and prone to injury. When fully grown they harden off and the velvet, its job done, withers and falls away. Once the velvet has been completely discarded, the antlers, which are pure bone, are said to be clean, this stage being reached shortly before the 'rut' or mating season. Later the antlers are shed and the cycle repeats itself, each succeeding pair of antlers being bigger, more branched and heavier until the deer reaches its prime.

The shape and size of antlers vary from species to species. The number of tines or points on the antlers of any specific animal is not necessarily indicative of the age of the deer carrying them, and antler growth is much more closely associated with the beast's habitat, the nutrimental value of its food, and genetics. The most accurate method of determining the age of deer is based on the eruption and wear of the animal's teeth.

There are two species of deer indigenous to the British Isles, the red deer (*Cervus elaphus*) and the roe deer (*Capreolus capreolus*). The latter comes into the Richmond Park story only briefly, so a short description will suffice. Today roe deer are common in large areas of Scotland, the Lake District, Northumberland, Yorkshire and much of the south of England but, with the exception of East Anglia, are scarce or absent in the area between. Nor are they found in Ireland and Wales. They frequent both deciduous and coniferous woodland, often where there is thick undergrowth, and the fringes of moorland. Although many attempts have been made to establish them in deer parks, they have never been very satisfactory as a park species.

The roe deer is a small animal with a rich red summer coat and a longer, softer, mouse-coloured winter coat. Their black noses and grizzled muzzles are distinctive features, and the antlers are short, upright, with seldom more than three points on each antler. The male is called a 'buck', the female a 'doe', and the young are 'kids'. Twins are frequent but triplets are not uncommon, and sometimes only a single kid is produced. As with most species of deer, they are born with a spotted coat. The herd instinct is not nearly so apparent in roe deer as it is in red and fallow, and for the most part they are seen either alone or in small groups. Only for a brief period in the thirteenth century did the roe deer enjoy the protection of the Forest Laws, and it was generally classified as 'a beast of the warren', inferior to red and fallow deer, on the grounds that its presence drove away other deer. In medieval times the 'beasts of the forest' included red and fallow deer as well as wild boar, all of which were protected by the Forest Laws.

The second of Britain's indigenous deer, the red deer, is well known, both in the wild and in the park. Popularly associated with the Scottish Highlands, the red deer's natural habitat is open woodland, and it was the wholesale destruction of forests in past centuries that drove them to the hill and mountainside. A mature red male, a stag, is a magnificent animal, measuring over a metre high to the shoulder and weighing 150 kg or more. Their antlers may have a span of almost a metre, as do those of Thetford Chase, and as many as forty-seven points, as had one stag in Warnham Park (Sussex) a few years ago. The stags of Richmond Park are more modest, seldom making more than sixteen or seventeen points. The

A Richmond Park stag

summer coat is a rich red-brown, lighter under the belly, the tail is short, the rump buff-coloured. The heavier winter coat is duller and more brown than red.

The antlers of a red stag are rounded in section. Immediately above the base of the antler of the adult animal is the first tine, or point, curving forward, known as the 'brow tine'. The second tine, again curved forward and usually shorter, is the 'bez' tine, and above that the longer but still forward-curving 'trez' tine. The shaft of the antler continues gently curving outward until it breaks up into the 'top points'. The antlers are shed in March and April, the larger stags in their prime being the first to lose them. Seldom are both shed simultaneously, and hours, or even days, can elapse between the loss of the first and second antlers. Almost immediately the new antlers start growing, first appearing as furry knobs, but within weeks developing into recognizable shape. In Richmond Park most of the stags are 'clean' by late August or early September. The first pair of antlers generally appear when the male is a yearling – that is, in his second year. Those are usually simple spikes, perhaps some 200–300 cm long, and the animal is then known as a 'knobber' or 'brocket', although the latter name is sometimes also applied to a stag in its third year. A stag reaches his prime when he is about five years old, and should remain in top condition for five or six years, perhaps longer, after which deterioration and ageing will gradually begin to show. If allowed to live out his natural life span, a stag may live for fifteen years or more, but by that time he will be but a shadow of his former self.

After the antlers are clean, the stag's neck thickens and a very definite mane develops. He is prone to wallowing in mud-holes, often coating himself with caked mud. He begins to smell strongly, a musty odour which can travel down wind quite some distance. It is at this time that he finds his adult voice, a leonine roar finishing with a series of deep coughs or grunts. The rut, or mating season, is approaching.

In Richmond Park the rut starts in early October and lasts for four to six weeks. The master stags return to traditional rutting stands, of which there are about a dozen, mostly concentrated on the west and south sides of the park, and will collect together a harem of twenty or more hinds. It is a period of intense excitement, and the calves, still at their mother's side, are obviously bewildered by the activity. Once he has gathered together his harem, the master stag must work hard to retain it, continually rounding up hinds which stray, and challenging the younger stags hanging around the edges of the group, hoping to cut out a hind or small group of hinds while the master stag's attention is engaged elsewhere. Much of the fighting and skirmishing is between the younger stags, and a challenging roar and brief charge from the master stag are usually sufficient to keep them in their place. A more serious encounter will occur from time to time as a stag approaching, or in his early prime, challenges the master stag. After spending some time moving parallel to each other, a few metres apart and at a tense walk, one or the other lowers his head, inviting contact. Heads clash, antlers lock and the animals try to throw each other off balance. It is a trial of strength, and eventually the weaker stag breaks off and flees. Serious injury rarely occurs and is usually accidental, not intentional.

During the rut the master stag seldom grazes and must be vigilant all the time. He quickly loses condition and weight and it is unlikely that he will remain with the hinds until the conclusion of the rut. Sooner or later he will retire and a second stag may take over, usually when the rut is well advanced. Alternatively small groups of hinds may be cut out by several of the younger stags, who are quick to take advantage of any opportunity that presents itself. In Richmond Park the peak of activity appears to be during the first few hours after dusk, and mating generally takes place at night. The stags are particularly vocal when the moon is full. Most hinds are served during the rut, but any which come into season late may be mated as late as February – a less than ideal situation, because the resultant calf will be late born and may not be sufficiently mature to survive its first winter.

The gestation period is about eight months, and the first park calves arrive in late May, the majority being born during the first two weeks of June. The hinds, usually accompanied by their previous year's offspring, return to traditional nursery areas to calve, one of which is Ham Cross Plantation between Richmond and Kingston Gates. Calving is normally achieved without difficulty, and the single calf is quickly, although not very steadily, on its feet. It is licked clean by the hind, who then instinctively eats the afterbirth so that predators (long extinct in this country) are not attracted to the vicinity. The calf, white spotted, spends most of the first few days of its life lying curled up amongst the grass and bracken fronds, so well camouflaged that it is almost invisible from a few metres. It is also, so it is said, scentless for the first two or three days of its life, and certainly dogs can pass close to a young calf, apparently completely unaware of its presence.

The hind will often be quite some distance from the calf, grazing, along with her offspring of the previous year, returning at intervals to suckle it. But they remain in communicating distance, a nasal bleat from the hind and a higher pitched, softer sound from the calf, which can, if it feels seriously threatened, also emit a shrill scream. The presence of a dog in the vicinity will bring mother and other hinds back at a trot. Graceful though they are, hinds returning to a threatened calf can look positively menacing. Although they will very seldom attack humans in defence of their young, they will go for dogs, straddling the dog and then kicking it

Hind with calf, Ham Cross Plantation

out from underneath them if they catch up with it. If kept on the leash or close at heel, dogs will not be attacked but several hinds may follow for quite some distance, in an aggressive style, if a dog is walked in the vicinity of a nursery area or a concealed calf.

Within a few days, perhaps a week, the calf will be seen more often with the mother, and by July herds of hinds, calves, yearlings and immature stags are often to be seen grazing together. By the time they are five or six weeks old, groups of calves will play together, very much after the fashion of lambs, being most active during the late evening and twilight hours. They start grazing within two hours of birth, and although hinds may still be lactating into the New Year, a calf is more or less self-reliant, as far as food is concerned, by late autumn. The pretty white spots are lost with the production of the first winter coat but vague spotting may be seen in the following and subsequent year's summer coat. As to sex ratio, there is no accurate record but, by and large, the number of female calves in the park which successfully survive their first year is approximately the same as that of male calves.

During the winter the mature stags are sometimes to be found together, sometimes in small groups. After they have shed their antlers they form a single herd and spend the summer grazing peacefully, usually in the northern area of the park. Hinds, calves and immature animals overwinter in a number of herds, each of which tends to remain in its own section of parkland, but from time to time two or more herds meet as they converge on the same grazing ground. Their movements are governed largely by grazing availability, prevailing weather conditions, and visitor disturbance.

Fallow deer (*Dama dama*) are not indigenous to the British Isles, although there is fossil evidence to show that a type of fallow was present in considerable numbers some 250,000 years ago. Larger than the European fallow of today, it was nevertheless similar in many ways and the species almost certainly died out during the last glaciation 100,000 years ago. The modern fallow may have been introduced by the Romans, from stock on the shores of the Mediterranean and Asia Minor, but it is not clear if they were imported in any quantity or even if they survived the Roman era. There is stronger evidence suggesting that the introduction was of comparatively recent origin, in the early Middle Ages, and that the Normans were probably responsible.[1] The Norman kings were great hunters; the fallow deer was highly regarded as a 'beast of the chase', and its venison was of good quality. It is an animal that thrives in captivity, thus an ideal species for the deer park.

Fallow deer are widely distributed throughout most of the British Isles, including Ireland, but are thin on the ground in Wales and absent from a few English and rather more Scottish counties. They are, outside the parks, feral animals, and it is likely that most populations are descendants of old forest herds and escapees from deer parks. In 1892 there were 390 English deer parks with fallow herds;[2] by 1974 fewer than a hundred remained.

Today the terminology used to describe fallow deer according to age and sex is straightforward. Until they are twelve months old, both male and female are called 'fawns'. The male, as a yearling and with its first set of antlers, simple spikes, is a 'pricket' and the female yearling a 'teg', although this name is not widely used. Thereafter the male is a 'buck' and the female a 'doe'. The ancient terminology is more complicated. The male was a 'fawn' during his first twelve months and a 'pricket' in the second. In his third year he became a 'sorel' or 'sorrell', the next year a 'sore' or 'soar', in the fifth year a 'bare buck'. In his sixth year he was a 'buck' and the following year, by which time he would be in his prime, the accolade of 'great buck' was bestowed. In fact, it is probably more accurate to relate those names to a given size and shape of antler rather than a given age. Some bucks with poor 'heads' (sets of antlers), for example, might never rise to the status of 'great buck'. The females had easier treatment, being fawns, tegs and finally does.

About the size of a domestic goat, the fallow deer is an elegant, graceful creature with soft, enquiring dark eyes. The coat colour varies from almost black, through a range of browns and chestnuts, sometimes spotted, sometimes not, to a near white or cream, a range of colour which adds to their attractiveness. The colour variations are broken down into four main groups, black, common, menil and white, but there are many intermediates. Black fallow have a sooty black summer coat, usually somewhat lighter underneath, and paler spots may occasionally be distinguished on close examination. The black variety is popularly supposed to have been imported from Denmark by James I (1603–25) but black fallow were present in Windsor Park as early as 1465.[3] They are also sometimes referred to as 'the old forest breed'. A chestnut summer coat, of variable shade with prominent white spots, followed by a darker, duller winter coat in which the spots are absent, or only just visible, identifies the common variety. The menil fallow deer retains its spots in the winter coat and has a Y-shaped convergence of spots on the haunches. White fallow deer start life with a gingery or light buff coat, and it is not until the following summer, when they are yearlings, that the off-white or creamy-coloured coat develops.

The Richmond Park fallow herds are of mixed colours. There are probably more menil than common, and the black and white groups are represented by only a few individuals of each. Does do not necessarily produce offspring of the same colour as themselves, and in those herds where the animals are all the same colour, for example the small white

Fallow bucks: common, black and menil

A buck cleaning its antlers of velvet, note the flies attracted by the now redundant velvet

herd in Bramshill Park, Hampshire, selective culling by colour is necessary to maintain their purity. Colour seems to have no association with
health, body weight and other qualities.

The adult buck's antlers are characterized by their palmation, the palm
flattening out above the trez tine, the rear edge of the palm broken up into
serrations known as 'spellers'. The bez tine is absent. The antlers sweep
outward and slightly backward and an individual antler, measured along
its surface may be some 70 cm in length and the palm 35–49 cm wide. As
with red deer, size varies greatly and is governed largely by habitat, the
nutrimental value of the available food, and genetics. Palmation may show
as no more than a flattening of the antler above the trez tine until the third
'head' but there can be considerable variation. The first set of antlers,
produced when the male is a yearling, are usually simple spikes. It is said
that, if the spikes show well above the erect ears and are evenly matched,
the chances are that the animal will subsequently produce good heads.
Richmond Park bucks cast their antlers rather later than the stags, the
older bucks at the end of April and the beginning of May, and the younger
animals later in that month. The antlers are clean of velvet by the end of
August.

There are several specific differences between the fallow and the red
deer rut, the most significant of which is that the fallow buck does not
round up and hold a harem in the manner of a stag. Instead, the does go to
him as they come into season. The fallow rut in the park is at its height
from mid October to early November, the activity slowly building up soon
after the antlers are clean. The necks of the bucks thicken and the Adam's
apple of the throat, always prominent in male fallow, becomes even more
prominent. The animal has suddenly become more muscular, masculine
and aggressive. Mature bucks take up positions in traditional rutting
stands, perhaps a quarter hectare in area, the boundaries marked by bucks
pawing scrapes in the ground onto which they urinate, thrashing vegetation with their antlers and anointing tree trunks and other permanent
structures with a secretion from scent glands situated below the eye.
Having established his territory, during which process he has probably had to fight and chase off other hopeful bucks, the buck attracts
the does to him by his pungent rutting odour and groaning: a deep,
belching groan which, on a still night, can be heard over a kilometre
away.

Rutting stands in Richmond Park are probably not nearly so well
defined as those in mature woodland and other areas. This may well be
because of visitor disturbance, combined with the varying use to which
some sections of the park have been put over the years. Nevertheless,
bucks return to the same area year after year. As with the stags, fighting
between bucks is a trial of strength, the weaker animal eventually breaking

An alert Fallow fawn in bracken

off the engagement and fleeing. Serious injuries are no more common than with the stags, but the park bucks are more prone to broken antlers. Bucks tend to be aggressive for a longer period than stags, and serious encounters, as opposed to sparring matches, are liable to occur well into the New Year, possibly over a doe which has come into season late. Rutting activity can be observed throughout the day but is at its peak at dusk and dawn.

After the rut, does, yearlings and immature bucks run in large groups or herds, sometimes almost a hundred strong. There are generally three to four of those winter groups, and experience suggests that they may be led by an aged but wily doe. The groups tend to remain each in an ill-defined area of the park, and there is some movement of animals from group to group. In late spring the large groups break up into smaller lots before the young are born in June and early July. The does generally, but not always, wander away from the herd, possibly accompanied by the previous year's offspring, if a female, to give birth, usually choosing a location with ample ground cover, often bracken. There are regularly used sites, for example in the wooded area immediately to the north of White Lodge and near Robin Hood Gate, but 'nursery areas' do not seem to be so well defined as those of the red deer. Birth is normally accomplished quickly and successfully, the fawn often being on its feet and making a few tottering steps within a short time of its arrival. Twins are rare, and only one confirmed case has been recorded in Richmond Park, when an aged doe, shot in March 1970, was found to be carrying apparently viable twin foetuses.[4]

With the exception of the black and the white varieties, fawns are well spotted when born and blend in with the surrounding vegetation. For much of their earlier life they remain still and concealed. When she is not attending to her offspring, the doe will move some distance away, grazing, possibly with her fawn of the previous year nearby. Communication between mother and youngster can be quite vocal, the doe bleating and the fawn mewing in reply. As the fawns grow older and are seen in groups, the conversation and chatter can be sometimes almost non-stop. Fawns tend to be more secretive than calves in the first weeks of their lives, and it may be late July and early August before groups can be observed at play, usually in the late evenings. Single youngsters, with the doe, may be seen by the end of June, however. The games that fawns play are, if anything, even more vigorous than those of calves, and they chase round at considerable speed, often punctuating their gallop with leaps and twists in the air. 'King of the castle' is an especially favoured game. With the approach of winter they sober up, so to speak, but a mild day in early spring encourages playful activity again. For no apparent reason a fawn will get up and set off at full gallop, in circles and figures-of-eight, through the herd. Others, encouraged, join in. Then, just as suddenly, the game ends.

Characteristic of fallow is the gait described as 'pronking'. This stiff-legged gait involves all four feet meeting the ground simultaneously, the animal erect, the tail held high. It is without doubt an alarm signal but is also used in play, sometimes being the precursor of a furious gallop, often in circles.

During the summer the does and fawns, together with immature males and females, remain in small groups. The mature bucks spend the summer months in bachelor groups, of which there are normally three, one in the south-west section of the park, the second in a rough triangle between White Ash Lodge, Bishop's Gate and Bog Lodge, and the third in and around the Sheen area. Fallow are more nervous and wary than red deer, a trait which makes them more vulnerable to involvement in traffic accidents. They are also great scroungers, especially the bucks who frequent the car-parks in summer, ready to accept illegally offered titbits and to tip up the litter baskets in the hope of finding a tasty morsel.

Despite their parallel life-cycles, fallow and red deer do not inter-breed, and experimental attempts to cross fallow and red by artificial insemination have proved unsuccessful. From time to time claims have been made of hybrid fallow-red, but those have usually been based on appearance and have not been confirmed. Some years ago a buck in the park carried antlers so similar to that of a stag that he was known as 'staghead'. But he was no hybrid – merely a fallow buck whose mother had forgotten to tell him to grow palmated antlers!

3

The Royal Venison Warrant

The tradition of distributing venison, or alternatively granting the right to take deer from a royal forest by authority of a royal warrant is an ancient one, the roots of which are embedded deep in English medieval history. Of William the Conqueror, the Anglo-Saxon Chronicle records that:

> He made great protection for the game
> And imposed laws for the same,
> That who so slew hart or hind
> Should be made blind.
> He preserved the harts and boars
> And loved the stags as much
> As if he were their father.[1]

The oppressive Forest Laws, together with the arbitrary rule of the earlier Norman kings, which offended baron and common man alike, eventually produced in retaliation the Magna Carta and the subsequent Charta Foresta. The latter contained a clause which granted to archbishops, bishops, earls and barons, when travelling through a royal forest on the King's business, the right to take one or two beasts for their own use, providing that the attention of the local forester (then an office of some importance in the administrative structures of the forests) was drawn to their presence.[2]

Other relevant charters involved the City of London. The City, which is a corporation by prescriptive right, probably evolved its corporative status in the twelfth century, and it secured from King John (1198–1216) the right to elect its own mayor and sheriffs annually. Henry I, by a charter made in the first year of his reign, granted and confirmed 'that the Citizens of London should have their Chases to hunt as well and as fully as their ancestors had that is to say in Chiltern and in Middlesex and Surrey'.

This right was confirmed, in turn, by Henry II, Richard I (1189–99), John and Henry III (1216–72).[3] The City's own hunt, the Common Hunt (later known as the Easter, or London Hunt), of which the Lord Mayor was *ex officio* Master, was established in the twelfth or thirteenth century.[4]

Some time between the end of the reign of Henry III and 1428, it seems that the Crown and the citizens of London came to an arrangement whereby the citizens apparently commuted their right to hunt in the royal forests, parks and chases in consideration of receiving from the Crown annually eighteen bucks and the same number of does. The warrant for those animals was granted to the officers of the City of London in the following proportion:

The Lord Mayor	Bucks 6	Does 6
The Sheriffs	Bucks 6	Does 6
The Recorder	Bucks 2	Does 2
The Chamberlain	Bucks 1	Does 1
The Town Clerk	Bucks 1	Does 1
The Common Sergeant	Bucks 1	Does 1
The City Remembrancer	Bucks 1	Does 1

One of the original warrants, granted in 1428 to Sir John Gedeny, Lord Mayor of London, is preserved in the British Museum. Written in Norman French, it is signed by the Archbishop of Canterbury, the Bishop of London and six others. The deer were to be supplied from the royal parks of Eltham and Windsor.[5]

It is doubtful if this *quid pro quo* arrangement, the annual grant of venison from the Crown in exchange for the City's hunting rights, was as straightforward as it seems. The Common Hunt was not finally disbanded until the mid nineteenth century and retained its own pack of hounds until 1807. In its later years the hunt met but once a year, in the royal forest of Epping (this was the last of the royal forests, disafforested by the Epping Forest Act of 1878, which placed it in the hands of the Corporation of the City of London) for a festive occasion at Easter. In 1633 there is record of the Common Hunt's man being present with the hounds at Kingston and Staines,[6] which suggests that the City still enjoyed hunting rights south of the Thames then. In a letter addressed to the Lord High Treasurer of England (Lord Burghley) by the Lord Mayor (Sir John Langley), dated 1577, the Lord Mayor wrote: 'We have them [the royal warrants] in respect of our privileges granted to the City to hunt in the Forests, Parks and Chases *in the County of Middlesex*'[3], which suggests that the City may have commuted only a proportion of their hunting rights in exchange for the grant of venison. It is possible that the grants were an attempt not to

A Royal Warrant, dated 1428, granting venison to the Lord Mayor of London

end the Corporation's hunting privileges but to clarify what were probably ill-defined rights by specifying the locations in which it could hunt, and perhaps the number of deer which the Hunt could take on any particular occasion.

Domestic State Papers of the sixteenth and seventeenth centuries are sprinkled with records of grants of venison by royal warrant. One such grant, authorized by James I (1603–25) in 1608, is of particular interest; not only does it include among the recipients certain offices of the Crown – 'the Farmers of our customs and the tellers of our Exchequer'[7] – which remain on the Royal Venison Warrant lists to this day; it also indicates that some recipients had the choice of either hunting and killing a specified number of deer personally or receiving their entitlement in the form of venison.

A normal practice in earlier centuries was the grant of 'fee deer' to senior park and forest officials. Fee deer were distinct from the grant of venison by royal warrant in that they formed part of the officials' emoluments, and they had the right to take an agreed number of deer annually for their own use, from the park or forest with which they were professionally associated. The practice continued until the nineteenth century, but early in the reign of Queen Victoria (1837–1901), by which time there remained only a handful of officials who qualified, the offices of those who received 'fee deer' were absorbed into what by then had become a consolidated Royal Venison Warrant.

The preparation of a consolidated warrant, bearing the offices and/or names of all who were privileged to receive venison from the royal parks and forests, and the number of deer each recipient was to receive, was first introduced in the mid eighteenth century, doubtless with the intention of easing the administrative burden of preparing and issuing numerous individual warrants every year. Two warrants, one for the buck season and the second for the doe season, were drawn up annually for the monarch's approbation and signature. Originally the Cofferer of the royal household (the Cofferer was the accounting officer of the household) was responsible for the administration of the consolidated warrant but, when this office was abolished in 1782, the department of the Lords of the Treasury took over the duty.

A copy of the warrant for the buck season of 1773 is preserved in the Public Records Office.[8] By then recipients had no choice but to accept their deer as venison (fallow venison was always used, being considered superior to that of other deer species), and the list shows that the officers of the City of London were to receive venison as had been the case during the fifteenth century. However, their quota had been cut; the number of carcasses destined for the City had been reduced from eighteen to fourteen in that year. A note on the warrant explains why. The Cofferer was unable to obtain a sufficient number of bucks from the parks and forests to satisfy the list, and some recipients had to be content with a lesser number of deer than they had been accustomed to. This problem – a shortfall in supply – was to dog the Royal Venison Warrant until the beginning of the twentieth century.

The great Offices of State, Church and Judiciary are all represented on the warrant. So, too, are the senior officers and servants of the royal household, together with a few junior posts such as the wardrobe-keeper at Hampton Court and the housekeeper at Kensington Palace. The 'farmers of our customs' of 1608 were now represented by the 'controllers' of the customs and petty customs, and the 'officers and under officers of the Exchequer' were no doubt the equivalent of James I's 'tellers of our Exchequer'. There were new faces too, among them the 'Directors of the South Sea Company, the Gov. and Direct. of the E. India Comp.' and 'The Post-master General'. The Duke of St Albans found his venison reduced from two animals to one that year. The first Duke, born in 1670, was the natural son of Charles II (1660–85), hence the right to royal venison. A hereditary title always held by the dukes of St Albans is that of the Grand Falconer of England.

The Cofferer distributed a total of 176 bucks that year; almost a hundred animals fewer than would have been the case had there been an adequate supply available to him. The bucks came from the New Forest Hampshire; Wychwood, Oxfordshire and Whittlewood Forests, Northamptonshire, Epping Forest, Essex, Dean Forest, Gloucestershire and Salsey Forest, Northamptonshire – virtually all that remained of the huge tracts of royal forests of an earlier era – and the royal parks of Windsor, (the great and the little parks), Richmond, Bushy, Hampton Court and Greenwich. Venison for the royal table was not, at this stage, included on the venison warrant, most of it probably coming from the fallow deer herd in Hyde Park, which park made no contribution to the warrant requirements.

'To the Commissioners of Our Woods, Forests, Land Revenues, Works and Buildings. This is to authorise and require you to Sign and Issue the proper Warrants to the Rangers and Keepers of our Forests and Parks to kill and deliver for the Service of Our Own Table and for the Lords and Others mentioned in the annexed List accustomed to Our Royal Favour a Doe or Does of this season according to the numbers placed against Their respective Names.
Given at Our Court at Windsor Castle this twenty fourth day of October 1839 In the third of our Reign
By Her Majesty's Command.'[9]

The number of deer required to satisfy this particular warrant was a staggering 756. And the sources of supply were diminishing – Dean and

Salsey Forests, together with Windsor Little Park, were no longer in a position to make a contribution. However, the total number of animals killed in the parks and forests probably showed little variation between 1773 and 1839 – what had happened was that those killed for the royal table, and as perquisites for the staff of the parks and forests (fee deer), had been added to the warrant list. The royal table alone accounted for sixty brace of fat bucks and a similar number of does, each year.

Difficulties in obtaining a sufficient number of deer to satisfy the requirements of the warrant remained a perennial problem. In addition, the Lords Commissioners of HM Treasury, then responsible for the administration of the warrant, had another worry to contend with: that of the poor quality of the venison, about which there had been many complaints. Positive measures were called for. In 1831 Edward Jesse, deputy surveyor of the royal parks and forests, was commissioned to carry out an investigation into the state of the fallow herds in all the parks and forests. Three years later a House of Commons Select Committee was set up to enquire into the perquisites of the rangers and keepers of the parks and forests, particularly fees paid to the keepers who delivered royal warrant venison to the various recipients.[10] The result was the publication, in 1838, of a set of regulations designed to overcome the problems of quantity and quality. A major requirement of the regulations was that the killing of *any* fallow deer for venison (in the parks and forests) could be authorized only through the medium of the royal warrant. Hence the inclusion, in the 1839 warrant, of the needs of the royal table, and the venison distributed to the park and forest staff.[11]

The regulations were successful in so far as there was an immediate improvement in quality. Quantity was another matter: the fallow herds of the parks and forests were simply not of sufficient size to produce the quantity of venison which the then voracious royal warrant demanded. The disafforestation of the New Forest (the Deer Removal Act of 1851) and of Wychwood and Whittlewood two years later was a considerable blow, their contribution having been about a sixth of the total amount of venison required. While some relief was gained by the removal of the officers of those forests from the warrant list, this was by no means sufficient to make up the deficit.

Something had to go. A number of individuals lost the privilege of receiving royal venison altogether, among them 'the Gentlemen and Magistrates in the vicinity of Windsor Great Park' who had been used to four deer each season, and the Mayor of Windsor, whose allocation had been a buck and a doe. Other recipients who had enjoyed more than one animal a season found their quota cut. A proposal was made to the City of London, suggesting that their allocation be reduced from eighteen animals to five (the reduction from eighteen to fourteen made by the

Cofferer in 1772 was of short duration only). The proposal drew an indignant response from the City Remembrancer, Edward Tyrrell, who successfully argued that the City of London's venison was a right and not a privilege and as such could not be arbitrarily reduced. Having won his point, Tyrrell agreed to accept twelve instead of eighteen deer, 'without prejudice to their legal right to the numbers which have for many hundreds of years been received by their Predecessors in Office and also without prejudice to the legal rights of the other Officers of the Corporation to whom no venison warrants had been allotted'. (Who those other officers were is not clear; the City officers who appeared on the fifteenth-century list had not been changed.)[3]

By the doe season of 1858 those measures had reduced the number of deer required for the warrant to 320.[12] Despite this, the fallow deer herds of the one remaining royal forest and the parks were still not large enough to cater for the demand. Attempts were made to increase the size of the herds in some parks; for example, large-scale land drainage was introduced into Richmond Park between 1856 and 1864, one of the recommendations made by Jesse following his 1831 investigation. Jesse had suggested that extensive land drainage would improve the pastures to a degree which would enable the fallow herds to increase from some 1,600 to 2,000.[10]

But it was not to be. 'There seems to be no probability of increasing the number of deer in the Royal Parks to an extent when the Warrants can be fully supplied', was the pessimistic view of one official in 1877.[11] This but two years after the Queen had graciously agreed to forgo, on a temporary basis, a proportion of the deer usually set aside for the royal table. Yet more pruning was done: the office of the Solicitor for the Affairs of Windsor Great Park disappeared from the list, and the Duke of Cambridge lost the venison he was used to receiving in lieu of rent for water laid on from his Coombe property (immediately to the south of Richmond Park) to Hampton Court Palace. The Duke was not in need of sympathy, however, for he continued to receive three deer each season by virtue of his office as penultimate Ranger of Richmond Park! More unfortunate were the park staff, who lost their nine does and nine bucks each year, in 1884.[8]

Not all of the venison which was set aside for the service of the royal table literally ended up there. Some was distributed among members of the household, presumably to those lesser mortals whose office was not considered to be of sufficient importance to attract a place on the warrant list. Nevertheless, during the long reign of Queen Victoria, venison dishes regularly appeared on the royal menu. Roast haunch of venison often appeared on the dinner menu at Buckingham Palace, Windsor Castle, Balmoral and Osborne House (Victoria's Isle of Wight retreat). Venison steaks were occasionally offered for the royal luncheon. Haunches of venison were sometimes served on special private occasions, an example being the dinner given by the Queen after the wedding of the Duke of Connaught and Princess Louise Margaret of Prussia on Thursday 13 March 1879. And on state occasions too. At a state banquet in St George's Hall, Windsor Castle, on Tuesday 21 November 1899, in honour of the German Emperor and Empress, 144 guests sat down to enjoy '*Venaison braisé à la Forestière*'.[13]

Freshly killed venison was also served out of season, quite legally. This was achieved by catching up selected bucks immediately after the rut and confining them in stalls, where they were fattened up by feeding. These 'stall-fed' animals were killed to provide venison during the close period between the end of the doe season (February) and the start of the fat buck season in June. Also available for killing out of season were 'haviours'; bucks which had been castrated in the early days of their life specifically for this purpose.

Yet another scheme designed to overcome supply and demand difficulties was made in 1893. The list of recipients was divided into two, and those offices considered to be of lesser importance were relegated to the second, smaller list. If, in any season, demand exceeded supply, the unfortunate office-bearers of the second list were to lose their venison in that season. Offices so relegated included those of senior civil servants, the officers of the City of London (with the exception of the Lord Mayor) and one or two of the less important hereditary offices.[14] In the event the precaution proved unnecessary: venison was beginning to lose its popularity on the high tables of the land. For the first time in centuries, the pressure exerted on the fallow herds of the royal parks by the Royal Venison Warrant was relaxing.

Probably for only the second time since the Middle Ages (the years of the Commonwealth being the first), the tradition of distributing venison by royal warrant was suspended in 1918. Food rationing in the First World War (1914–18) was the cause; George V (1910–36) considered that it would be unreasonable to continue distributing venison in this way when the country was in the grips of a food and meat shortage (venison from the royal parks was sold to the Central Meat Marketing Board during the war years as a contribution to the nation's depleted larder).[15] Although it was reinstated in 1920, the Royal Venison Warrant was never to regain its former glory. In the summer of 1921 the King indicated that he no longer required deer to be specially fed (stall-fed bucks) for the royal table,[16] the demands of which by then reduced to fewer than thirty deer in most seasons. Between the wars a modest eighty animals each season were enough to satisfy the needs of the warrant,[17] which was, perhaps, just as well, because the only remaining sources of

Inside Sheen Gate, 1941. Sheen Cross Plantation is in the background (originally published in *Picture Post*)

supply were the royal parks of Richmond, Windsor, Hampton Court and Bushy.

Only a few years later, war was again responsible for the suspension of the warrant. In the spring of 1940 George VI (1936–52) approved this action, and on this occasion the suspension was to last for nine years. When it was revived, it was to a very different set of circumstances than had previously existed. During the Second World War (1939–45), much greater use of the royal parks for military and agricultural purposes was made than had been the case in former times of national emergency. The deer herds were reduced to a mere handful of animals as a consequence, leaving a nucleus of deer sufficient only to allow the herds to be rebuilt after the war. An exception was Windsor Great Park, most of which was left under the plough much longer than the other parks, and the deer herds of the Great Park were not rebuilt; instead the few remaining deer were dispersed elsewhere in 1950.[18]

It was the Remembrancer of the City of London, appropriately, who wrote to the Ministry of Works,[18] then responsible for the management of London's royal parks, reminding the Minister of the City's *right* to venison from the parks. After much internal discussion the Minister recommended that the custom of distributing venison by royal warrant should be revived, to preserve the ancient rights and traditions associated with it. To prevent the tradition becoming a burden on the remaining deer herds, he also recommended that each season the distribution be restricted to a single haunch of venison per recipient (if he or she accepted the invitation to partake of the right or privilege), with four haunches reserved for the royal table. The recommendations were accepted, the warrant was re-introduced in time for the doe season of 1949, and a small part of the nation's heritage was preserved.

The post-war warrant is a mixture of precedent and principle. In 1953 a Ministry of Works official described the lists – for there are still two – as 'containing some names of people who get the venison by ancient right and who have some connection with it and those such as Cabinet Ministers who appear on the List because it seems proper to put them there'! In fact names are not mentioned on the warrant, only the offices being described. The great of Offices of State, Church and Judiciary are represented, and the officers of the City of London still enjoy their right to venison. The Lords Commissioners of HM Treasury – the Government Whips – appear on the lists, no doubt because of their earlier involvement with the administration of the warrant. Other offices included are those of the Chairman of the Board of HM Customs and Excise, the Governor of the Bank of England, and the Secretary of the Crown Estate Commissioners. The Civil Service is represented by the Permanent Secretaries. Ancient offices such as the Master of the Horse, the Grand Falconer of

England, the Captains of the Queen's Bodyguard of the Yeomen of the Guard and the Honourable Corps of Gentlemen-at-Arms are not forgotten. In all 101 offices appear on the warrant.

Not all offices which were in receipt of grants of venison in pre-war years appeared on the post-war list. The Dean and Chapter of Windsor was one casualty – probably because of the demise of the Windsor Great Park herds. The Dean claimed a right to venison from the royal parks and forests by a grant made by Edward III.[18] It has not been possible to confirm this claim, and no mention of venison is made in the foundation charter of the College of St George, Windsor Castle, or in subsequent grants. However, the Chapter's audit books of 1751–2[19] do record the payment of venison fees, and a few years later the Chapter was receiving venison by virtue of royal warrant.

Other casualties were the Manor of Richmond and the Corporation of Kingston, both of which had enjoyed royal venison in bygone years by ancient right or privilege. On the resumption of the warrant in 1949, it had been decided that no additions would be made to the lists, no matter how justified the case – this to protect the herds against the pressures of yesteryear which the warrant had placed on them. The only exception which has been made was the restoration of the privilege to the mayors of Richmond and Kingston – no doubt because of their proximity to, and association with, the parks which now provide all the warrant venison.

Deer are no longer specifically kept or slaughtered for the service of the warrant. The haunches which are distributed are from animals which in any case have to be culled for deer-management purposes. Two-thirds of the venison are supplied by Richmond Park, the remainder from Hampton Court and Bushy parks – this in direct proportion to the relative size of the fallow herds of each park.

The grant of venison from the royal parks (and in earlier years the forests) is not a gratis gift. As early as 1236 the warden of Windsor Forest claimed expenses for hunting eight deer and transporting them to Westminster Abbey as a gift from the king. Some years later his colleague in the New Forest made a similar claim for hunting, salting and delivering venison to the king's son.[20] In 1537 Princess Mary, daughter of Henry VIII, paid 3s. 4d. to the keeper of the Little Park at Richmond, for a doe he had delivered to Richmond Palace.[21] During the Commonwealth, when Richmond Park was in the care of the City of London, the keepers received fees on several occasions for delivering venison for 'the Lord Protector and Common Councils'.[22] In 1780 George III (1760–1820) instructed the Board of Green Cloth (essentially the management board of the royal household, presided over by the Lord Steward and consisting of senior officers of the household) to pay the keepers of the parks and forests, who were obliged to deliver venison for the royal table personally,

10s. 6d. for each buck, and 6s. 8d. per doe, delivered punctually and in good condition. Two years later, in a second instruction, which increased the reward or fee paid to the keepers, there is a direct reference to 'the ancient fee' in respect of venison from the parks and forests.[23]

Early in the nineteenth century the Board of Green Cloth complained about the quality of the venison. 'The badness of the venison was notorious, the feed being overstocked by other animals for private emolument and the deer when killed were shamefully cut and robbed not only of the fat but also of a considerable proportion of the carcass.'[24] The complaint was not confined to the venison supplied for the royal table; it extended to all venison from the parks and forests. Since the parks and forests were beyond the jurisdiction of the Lord Steward, he laid the complaint before the Commissioners of HM Woods, Forests and Land Revenues, the result of which was the setting up of the House of Commons Select Committee in 1834.

The Committee made a number of recommendations, including a proposal that fees should no longer be paid to the keepers but directly to the Office of Woods etc. The King, William IV (1830–37), approved the proposal. The Board of Green Cloth, not having been consulted by the Select Committee prior to the King's approval being sought, objected,[24] on a point of protocol. William IV had inadvertently interfered with the authority granted to the Lord Steward by the Sovereign's Warrant, which was at that time issued by the monarch at the beginning of every reign; he should have consulted the Board before formally approving the proposal. Having made its point, the Board withdrew its objection in 1837, and the proposal became part of the regulations governing the distribution of royal park and forest venison the following year.

It was not the Select Committee's intention to deprive the keepers of the benefit of the fees. The 'Woods and Forests Fund' was intended to provide for the families of the keepers in cases of sickness and death, and for good-conduct rewards to keepers who performed their duties exceptionally well. But the fund was, in the event, not to be administered as the Committee had desired. Although the Treasury, which controlled it, paid annuities and gratuities in a few cases, they refused to accept the pension concept and ruled that no claims would be admitted in respect of keepers appointed after 16 November 1838. Thereafter the fees were appropriated by the Exchequer as 'extra receipts'. Since this was contrary to the arrangements which had been sanctioned by the monarch, it was agreed that fees should no longer be paid in respect of royal table venison but that they would remain payable by all other recipients of royal warrant venison.

The fees were set at £1. 6s. od. per buck, and 16 shillings per doe, exclusive of carriage costs, which the recipients were also expected to pay. It was not until the warrant was revived after the Second World War that the fees were adjusted, by which time only haunches were being distributed, and they attracted a fee of 10 shillings for a buck haunch and 5 shillings for that of a doe. The onus of meeting carriage charges remained with the recipients. A few years later the fees and carriage costs were amalgamated, and an equal fee, inclusive of carriage costs, was introduced for both buck and doe venison. And so it remains today, with adjustments being made from time to time to keep pace with inflation. Albeit in disguised form, the ancient fee still lives on.

The Park – the Beginning

Deer parks associated with royalty were not new to north Surrey. A park in the Manor of Shene is first mentioned in 1293. The manor formally reverted to the Crown in the early fourteenth century (it had previously been owned by Henry I), and by 1437 a second park had been created, adjacent to the palace which had been developed by the riverside. The location of the original park is not known, but the second one was to the north-west of the palace.[1] It was probably this park of which John Bury, Yeoman of the Hall, was made keeper in 1440. Known as 'le Newe Park of Shene Co Surrey', it was stocked with fallow deer, because the grant of the keepership of the park included 'seven acres of meadow by Chertsey Bridge Co Middlesex to feed the King's fallow deer within the said park in winter time'.[2]

Shene Park was the subject of a letter written by Queen Margaret of Anjou, wife of Henry VI (1422–61), probably before the disruptions of the Wars of the Roses (1455–85). 'By the Queen. To my lords squier and ours, J. D. Keper of Shene Park or his Depute there,' wrote the Queen. 'Trusty and welbeloved. For as muche as we suppose that in short tyme, we shall come right negh unto my lords menoir of Shene, we desire and praye you hastly that ye will kepe against our resortinge thedor, for oure disporte and recreation, two or iii of the grettest bukkes in my lord's parc there, saving alweyes my lord's oune commandment there in presence. As we trust etc.'[3] Which of the two parks this was is not clear.

At the end of the fifteenth century the palace was destroyed by fire, and Henry VII (1485–1509), the first monarch of the Tudor dynasty, built in its place a new palace of some magnificence. He also changed the name of Shene to Richmond, having been the Earl of Richmond before becoming King.

With the palace built and the Court re-established, royal entertainment was carried out on a grand scale. A contemporary writer has left a vivid description of a hunt held there in 1503. The event was preceded by splendid pageantry, including an archery display by the Yeomen of the Crown and the King's Guard. 'Afterward,' the account continues 'the Kinge's Highness ledde the estraingers into his p'ke adjoyning unto the rehersid manour of Richemond, and there causid wanlacs to be made and the dere to be brought about, and gave the estraingers fre chace wt bowe and bownde. And there the Earl of Hispayne strake a dere wite his crossebowe, and great slaughter was of veneson by the seid estraungers and brought unto the quarry. The fleshes thereof the King's G'ce distributed and gave unto the Espanyards to do therwt ther will and pleasur.'[4] In which of the parks this slaughter took place is not specified.

After 1525, Henry VIII used the palace at Richmond infrequently, preferring Hampton Court. His daughter Mary was often in residence, and her household accounts for 1537 recorded a payment of 3s. 4d. to the keeper of the 'Little Park' for bringing a doe from that park to the palace.[5] Presumably the 'Little Park' was one of those associated with the palace, but which one it was cannot be established. James I (1603–25) is credited with making a third park, adjacent and to the north of the 1437 park, part of which is probably the Old Deer Park of today.[1]

There was yet another park in the area in which the Crown had an interest. This was Putney Park, sometimes also called Mortlake. That this, too, was a deer park is evident from annual grants of £15 'to buy hay for the deer' to Sir Charles Howard, who was Master of the game in that park during the reign of James I. Charles I, in 1626, granted the park to Sir Richard Weston (later Earl of Portland) who in 1635 was granted a licence to impark an additional 182 hectares. Following the death of the Earl in 1637, his son (of whom more later) disposed of some of the family estates. It was from this source that the King obtained the largest proportion of that section of Richmond Park which lies on the east side of the Beverley Brook.[6]

The first recorded transaction involving Richmond Great, or New Park – the name by which it was first known, no doubt to distinguish it from the riverside parks – was in 1630, when one Edward Manning was granted a warrant 'for payment of an imprest . . . for railing in coppices, making ponds, and cutting lawns in the New Park at Richmond, and bringing a river to run through the same'.[7] There is no evidence or record to suggest that the river in question was the Beverley Brook, which bisects the park on the east side, flowing south to north through it to join the Thames at Mortlake, nor evidence or record of any ponds having existed along that section of the Beverley Brook which passes through the park. More probably the 'river' was the water-course which rises from natural springs in the west of the park, and is shown on the Enclosure map prepared for Charles I.[8] The Pen Ponds first come to notice in John Rocque's *Survey of*

London, made between 1741 and 1745.[9] The survey shows that they were very much the same, in outline and area, as they are today, though they were then known as canals. There are references to 'the Great Pond' early in the park's history,[10] and it may well have been that the ponds, as they are shown in Rocque's *Survey*, were developed from those for the construction of which Edward Manning was paid in 1630, and that they were made as fishponds after the medieval style of park design.

A substantial portion of the 2,400 acres (1,000 hectares) which were enclosed within the park walls was already Crown land, but there were also significant areas of common land, and Clarendon recorded that 'Many gentlemen and farmers had good houses and good farms intermingled with those wastes.'[11] Obtaining the privately owned lands and commons proved difficult because of local resistance, and although the King eventually succeeded in buying out landlord and commoner, he did so at the expense of personal popularity. It was against the earnest advice of his advisers and ministers that he conducted the purchases. According to Manning and Bray, 'Laud Archbishop of Canterbury, Juxon Bishop of London, and the Lord Cottington then Chancellor of the Exchequer being solicited from day to day (by the people of the neighbourhood) could no longer resist their importunity; and did warmly represent to the King how impolitic a step he was taking.'[12]

The way in which the King won possession of those private and common lands had more than a hint of medieval flavour. An account of the enclosure of the park, penned in the nineteenth century, is brief and succinct: 'Charles enjoyed hunting with hereditary zest, and had sacrificed to this passion the long-sacred immunities of British property. He enclosed Richmond Park with as little ceremony as the first Norman conqueror showed to his Saxon slaves, for the greater convenience of having red as well as fallow deer so close at hand.'[13]

The undulating land contained within the two-metre-high brick wall built by Charles I around his park would have been familiar to a medieval park-maker. It was probably well furnished with trees, particularly on the higher ground, with English oak predominating. The large stretches of waste and common land no doubt carried a poor-quality pasture, with extensive patches of scrub, bracken and furze (gorse). Low-lying land would, in the main, lie wet and marshy, much as it does today. And there were areas of cultivated land, even fields, the lines of which can still be seen in the form of broken lines of ancient oak trees which correspond with the old field boundaries, shown on the Ordnance Survey Sheet[14] of the park, around Bog Lodge in the north. Other indications of agricultural cultivation, possibly dating from the Middle Ages, are 'ridge and furrow' lands near Kingston Gate, and on the east side of the Beverley Brook, on some of the fairways of the park's two (public) golf courses.

Left: The Upper Pen Pond   51

London Clay forms the basic geological foundation of the park. Where undisturbed, it is a blue-grey silty clay to within five metres of the surface, above which depth it breaks down to a weathered brown clay which, in low areas, outcrops to the surface. Sand and gravel occur at three main elevations, and those deposits, or terraces, form the sub-soil strata over much of the higher land. Gently sloping London Clay banks provide the link between the terraces and low-lying ground, the clay beds of which have been eroded by water courses and streams. Top soils range from sandy to clay loams and, with the exception of areas which have been subjected to past cultivation, tend to be thin, acid and of low fertility. Except on high ground, natural drainage is poor.

The highest point in the park, at fifty-seven metres above sea level, is a man-made mound in the gardens of Pembroke Lodge. Popular legend has it that it was on this mound that Henry VIII waited, on the morning of

An ancient oak on the edge of Barn Wood

19 May 1536, for the sound of the signal-gun from the Tower of London signifying that Anne Boleyn, his second wife, had been duly executed. A dramatic story perhaps, but one which historical evidence suggests is improbable. Nevertheless, it is known as King Henry VIII Mound and has been since 1754,[15] if not earlier (there is a reference to King Henry VII Mound in Richmond Park in Treasury Books of 1698).[16] On the Enclosure map it is called 'The King's Standinge', and it certainly would have provided Charles I with an excellent vantage point of the park. The mound is much older than the park, and Edward Jesse, writing in 1835,[17] claims 'that there can be no doubt that this mound was formerly a British barrow. It has been opened, and a considerable deposit of ashes was found in the centre of it.' Today the mound affords a magnificent panorama to the west, and a vista, cut through Sidmouth Plantation to the north-east, frames St Paul's Cathedral ten miles away.

The 'Free Board', or 'Freebord', a strip of land 16½ feet (one rod, pole or perch) wide on the external side of the boundary wall, is absent only from those sections of the park perimeter which adjoin neighbouring Crown land. Originally it permitted external accesss to the wall, for building and repair work, without the need to cross adjacent, privately owned land; today it serves much the same purpose. In earlier years there may have been a barrier, in the form of a hedge or perhaps a fence, on the outer edge of the freebord as a defence against deer escaping through a breach in the wall.

Although Clarendon implies that there were a number of 'good houses' within the area of the park about the time of the Enclosure, there were probably only two. One of the parcels of land purchased by Charles I was an estate and manor house at Petersham in the west of the Park, and this house, Petersham Lodge, was enclosed with the park.[18] The second house was located on the west side of what is now Spanker's Hill Plantation, and in November 1637 a warrant for the payment of £290, spent on either the construction or the repair of this dwelling, was issued.[19] There was no great house or palace within the park, and the two houses were granted to the two joint keepers, appointed by Charles I in 1636. Further shades of a medieval-type deer park.

The two keepers were 'Keepers of the Lodges and Walks' (divisions of a forest or a park), as opposed to 'the Keeper of the Park'. The medieval tradition of granting the keepership of a royal park to a nobleman or a high-ranking member of the Court or household was one which survived until the beginning of this century; indeed it is kept alive today for HRH the Duke of Edinburgh is Ranger of Great Windsor Park. Charles I selected Jerome, Earl of Portland, the son of Sir Richard Weston of Mortlake Park, as 'Keeper of His Majesty's New Park near Richmont' in June 1637.[20] It was not until some years later that the title of the office was changed to Ranger; there is reference to the 'Cheife Raynger' in 1650.[21] Originally a ranger was an official of the forest, first mention of which is made in the mid fourteenth century. What his duties then were is not clear, but later the ranger was responsible for the 'purlieu', an area of land adjacent to a royal forest which at one time had been part of the forest. One of his duties involved driving deer which had strayed into the purlieu, where they were not protected by Forest Law, back into the forest, where they were protected.[22] Even later the office seems to have become a sinecure, and it was apparently not associated with parks until the mid seventeenth century.

The Keepers of the Lodges and Walks were Lodowick Carlile and Humfry Rogers. The former was appointed keeper of Petersham Lodge and Walk, and Rogers of Hartleton Lodge and Walk. Little is known of the personal life of Rogers, but that of Carlile (variously spelt Carlisle,

Carlell, Carliel etc.) has been documented and provides an insight into the status of keepers during the seventeenth century. Carlile's father, Robert, a Scotsman whose family came from Broadkirk (or Bridekirk) in Dumfriesshire, was master huntsman to James I and accompanied the King to England in that capacity when James acceded to the English throne in 1603.[23] Robert Carlile returned to Scotland in 1608 to purchase some hounds from Dumfriesshire for the King, and made the same journey, for the same purpose, in 1628, by which time Charles I was the monarch.

Lodowick was twenty-four years old when he married Joan, daughter of William Palmer, paymaster to the staff of St James's Park, in 1626. That Palmer's position was of one of some standing is evident from his daughter's marriage licence, on which he is described as being of 'St James Park gent'. Lodowick himself was a minor Court official as well as keeper of Petersham Lodge and Walk, being 'Gentleman of the Bows' to Charles I, and 'Groom of the Chamber' to the Queen. He was, furthermore, a minor poet and dramatist, and some of his plays were performed at Court. His first play, *The Deserving Favourite*, he dedicated to William Murray, father of the Countess of Dysart of Ham House, and Thomas Cary. In the prologue of a later play, *The Passionate Lovers* (published in 1655), there is a direct reference to his position as keeper in Richmond Park:[24]

> Most here knows,
> This Author hunts, and hawks, and feeds his Deer,
> Not some, but most fair days throughout the year.

In view of this talent, it is not altogether surprising that a later member of the Carlile family was also adept with the pen. This was the Rev. Alex Carlyle, minister of Inveresk (Scotland), who died in 1805 and who wrote, as 'Jupiter' Carlyle, interesting and valuable memoirs of his life and times.[23]

Joan Carlile, too, had artistic talent to offer. She was one of England's earliest women professional portrait painters and enjoyed the patronage of the Court. Two of her works are worthy of note. Her *Group of Figures at a Stag Hunt* (oil on canvas), painted about 1649, is presumed to be of a scene in Richmond Park and hangs at Lamport Hall, Northamptonshire. The second work, also oil on canvas, and painted at about the same time, depicts Sir Lionel Tollemache, who later became Ranger of the Park, his wife (later the Countess of Dysart) and sister-in-law. This picture hangs at Ham House, Surrey.[25]

State papers of 23 February 1637 record the authorization of a payment of £100 to Carlile and Rogers for 'pease, tares and hay, for the red and

Group of figures at a stag hunt (attributed to Joan Carlile)

fallow deer in the Great Park at Richmond',[26] a sum which would then have bought a very considerable quantity of these commodities. It seems reasonable to speculate, in the absence of specific records, that the two keepers were appointed prior to the enclosure of the park, with instructions to feed as many deer as possible in the locality, so that they were attracted to within the area of the park before the last gaps in the boundary walls were closed. That there were deer to be so enticed is likely, escapees from the several deer parks stocked with fallow in the vicinity. Another possible source of fallow deer is Putney Park, which was owned by Jerome, Earl of Portland, the first keeper of the King's new park. There is a hint, too, of the presence of red deer in the surrounding countryside. In 1636 the Marquis of Hamilton, Master of the Horse, reported to the King that 'the roe deer escaping out of the Old Park at Wimbledon had been killed in the woods attached and that red deer came from Windsor Forest and Far Oak into these parts . . .'[27] (Windsor Forest was then some 24,000 acres – 10,000 hectares – in area.)

In April 1640 Robert Jones Esq., Master of HM Toils, and his two assistants, the Yeomen of the Toils (toils were strong nets of considerable length, used for catching up live deer), were paid £2,121. 16s. 4d., in respect of their wages and expenses in catching up an unspecified number of red deer in eight walks of Windsor Forest, and transporting them to 'HM new park at Richmond.'[28]

Having created and stocked his park, the King made good use of it, hunting regularly at Richmond until the start of the Civil War in 1642. Charles I was soon a prisoner, but even as such was permitted to hunt from time to time. On 28 August 1647, eighteen months before his execution, 'The King was a hunting in New Parke, killed a Stag and a Buck; afterwards dined at Syon.' And a few days later, 'The Duke of York, with the Lords, were hunting in the new Parke at Richmond where there was good sport – the King cheerefull and much company there.'[29]

Charles I was executed at Whitehall in January 1649. The Commonwealth was established, and Parliament quickly passed Acts abolishing the trappings of royalty, and for the sale of Crown lands – with few exceptions, one of which was Richmond New Park, which was gifted to the Mayor and Commonalty and Citizens of London, in recognition of the assistance given by the City to Cromwell during the Civil War. The Earl of Portland, a Royalist, lost his office as ranger of the park, but the two keepers, Carlile and Rogers, were retained.

In the years leading up to the Interregnum, the Carliles found themselves in financial straits, no doubt because the King was, by then, in no position to pay his keepers regularly. To make ends meet, they ran Petersham Lodge as a high-class lodging house, entertaining a succession of noblemen, squires and others of similar standing, most of them with

Royalist leanings. They were evidently popular hosts and provided for their guests 'all nessessaryes but linning'.[24]

Because of his Court connections and his activities as a lodging-house keeper, it is perhaps surprising that Carlile was retained as keeper during the Commonwealth period. The City of London, however, were required by Parliament to maintain the park to a high standard during their period of ownership (see Chapter 1, p. 19) and may well have considered it advisable, in the light of their responsibilities, to make use of the expertise of both Carlile and Rogers. Other considerations may also have been involved. Joan Carlile's cousin was married to John Thurloe, Cromwell's Secretary of State. And the Carliles were acquainted with the Countess of Dysart of Ham House, a shrewd and ambitious lady who was reputed to have had influence with Cromwell. The Carliles did, in fact, leave the park for a brief period in 1654, when they moved to Covent Garden, then the artists' quarter of London, presumably in order to further Joan's career as a portrait painter. They returned to Petersham Lodge in the summer of 1656, and Carlile does not appear to have relinquished his office as keeper during their absence.[25]

During the Commonwealth years, the keepers each received an annual salary of £50, and their income was augmented from time to time by payments for billeting soldiers in the park, and other similar services. There is evidence to suggest that they were able to swell their income even more by indulging in a certain amount of private enterprise. From 1652 onward, the City obliged them to pay an annual rent of £220 for 'Pannage [the right to pasture swine in woods] agistments [rent paid for grazing cattle on pasture land] grass hay gorse or furrs bushes or yearly proffitts groweing being or made off in out off or upon the said Park or grounds or any part thereof (excepting the goeing depasturing Feeding and keeping of 1300 Fallowe deere and 200 Red deere in upon the said Park yearly etc.)'.[30]

This suggests that the Park was well stocked with deer in 1652 and later, but this may not necessarily have been the case in 1649. On 14 February 1650 the Court of Aldermen for the Corporation of the City of London appointed a committee of several aldermen, together with a Major Salway, to negotiate with Mr Carey Rawleigh (or Raleigh) of Kempton Park (once a royal park) concerning the purchase of deer 'for the better storeing of New Park'. Agreement was reached by May 1650 whereby 'that for every head of Deare as well male as female younge or old that shalle safely delivered into the Carraiges upon the place and adjudged by Mr. Carlile and Mr. Rogers to be sound and well condicioned shalbee pd. to the said Mr. Raleigh or his assignes twenty shillings apeece'. Mr Raleigh was to pay the transport costs but the committee undertook responsibility for 'all Damages and mischances that shall happen to the said Deere or any of them between Kempton Parke and Newparke'.[31]

The City Chamberlain was instructed by the Court of Aldermen to pay Mr Raleigh for the deer delivered to date on 9 May 1650. At the same time they instructed the committee 'due take in as many more good deere as they can for XX's a deere providing the same exceede not two hundred and fiftee'. In the event, the number of deer finally delivered was much lower, since the Chamberlain's Cash Account records that Carey Rawleigh was paid 20 shillings a head for a total of 133 fallow deer.[31] (The deer herds of Kempton Park, to digress for a moment, were finally dispersed during the second half of the nineteenth century, and the racecourse was established there in 1889.)

Deer were also purchased by the City, for the park, in 1650–51, and again three years later. The supplier on those occasions was a Captain Ditcher. On 1 May 1651 the City Chamberlain was instructed to pay Captin Ditcher £50, being 'part of monies due for deer delivered by him to the New Park'.[32] The total number of deer supplied by the Captain is not specified, nor is the species or original source identified. It seems likely that they were fallow, and a significant number were probably involved. The cost of deer bought from yet another source, 'the great Parke of Nonsuch' (at Cheam, Surrey), was £81, this purchase being made in 1651–2.[33] Originally acquired for the Crown by Henry VIII, the park and palace were sold in 1649 by Act of Parliament but returned to the Crown at the Restoration. Charles II then granted Nonsuch to his mistress the Duchess of Cleveland (whose grandson sold the property to the Duke of Grafton in 1730).

This restocking programme suggests that the City was living up to its obligations to Parliament in respect of the care of the park. On 19 April 1653 the Common Council appointed a committee of aldermen and sheriffs 'to Mannage the New Parke and all the Cityes Interest therein to the honour and best advantage of the Maior Cominalty and Citizens of this Citty According to the Act of Parliament graunting the same'.[34] Five years later yet another committee was set up 'to take a viewe of New Parke and the deere there', and Mr John Michel, a Richmond attorney, was appointed as 'Clerke to the said comitee',[24] further verification that the City was indeed taking its responsibilities seriously.

The deer herds, however, were not maintained solely for their ornamental value. Parliament and the Council of State, despite their puritanical front, were not averse to the occasional joint of venison! On one of several occasions the Court of Aldermen, on 13 September 1651, instructed 'that Mr. Remembrancer doe presently goe from this Court and require the Keepers of the New Parke to kill in that Parke a brace of fatt stags of this season and deliver the same for the use of the Parliament and Councell of State on Munday morning next'.[35] On another, 'Mr. Chamblen' was instructed, on 7 November 1654, to pay to the keepers fees of £7. 6. 8d for 'venison killed in the said Parke for entertainment of the Lord Protect and the Comon Councill.'[36]

Although some woodland was felled for timber sales in the Commonwealth period, and later some difficulty was experienced in the maintenance of the boundary walls,[37] the City seems to have looked after Richmond Park with some efficiency during its eleven years of ownership. There is no record of any significant change or alteration having been made. The park, which the City (no doubt with an eye to its future prosperity) was quick to return to the Crown on the restoration of the monarchy in 1660, was probably in better repair, and with a larger stock of deer, than was the case when it was last in Crown hands.

5

The Park – 1660–1727

Charles II (1660–85) with enthusiasm set about the very considerable task of repairing and replenishing with deer the royal forests and parks, for not all had survived the Civil War and Commonwealth as successfully as Richmond. Red and fallow deer were imported from Germany, and elsewhere on the Continent, for restocking the forests of Windsor and Sherwood, amongst others. Landed gentry and major landlords whose parks and estates had been fortunate enough to escape the worst attentions of the Roundheads, were quick to offer deer from their lands, no doubt with the intention of demonstrating their loyalty to the Crown. The King was just as quick to accept the offers, and there are many records of the transfer of deer in the early years of his reign. No doubt because the City had left the park well stocked, few of the deer were destined for Richmond. But some did, because on 7 March 1662 a warrant was issued authorizing the payment of £300 to Sir Lionel Tollemache, Bart., for feeding an unspecified number of deer 'lately brought to Richmond Great Park for the King's disport and recreation'.[1]

With the restoration of the park to the Crown came the restoration of the office of Ranger. There were two contenders. Sir Daniel Harvey (nephew of William Harvey, the physician who first described the circulation of blood in the human body) had been knighted by Charles II in 1660. He lived locally, being Lord of Coombe (Neville) Manor to the south of the park, and was married to Elizabeth, only daughter of Edward, the second Lord Montagu of Boughton (Northants).[2] The second contender was none other than the Countess of Dysart, whose claim was based on the fact that areas of the Dysart estates had been incorporated into the park by Charles I and that her father, William Murray, had been Groom of the Bedchamber to that King.[3] In the event, Charles II favoured the Countess and her husband, Sir Lionel Tollemache, who were appointed joint Rangers in July 1660.[4] The unfortunate Sir Daniel

Harvey was granted, probably by way of compensation, the reversion of the custody of the park, after the Countess of Dysart and Sir Lionel.[5]

At the same time the two keepers, Carlile and Rogers, had their appointments reconfirmed, Carlile as keeper of Petersham Lodge and Walk, and Rogers of Hartleton Lodge and Walk. By September 1662, Carlile was being assisted by his son; Treasury Books record the payment of £50 per annum to Lodowick Carlile and James Carlile, his son, 'as fee for the custody and keeping of His Majesty's house or lodge at Petersham, within His Majesty's Great Park near Richmond, together with the walk in the same park to the said house belonging, as by letters patent of 1660, Sep.27'.[6] Carlile was also reinstated as 'Gentleman of the Bowes in ordinary to his Majesty' and was granted an annuity of £200 by Charles II,[2] in addition to the £50 per annum he earned as keeper of Petersham Lodge and Walk.

Rogers surrendered his office in November 1661, and Carlile and his son followed suit two years later. There is evidence[7] to suggest that Sir Lionel Tollemache had sought to curtail the rights of the keepers to make profits out of the park, an arrangement which they had made during the Commonwealth period. Whether or not there was a connection between this and the resignation of the keepers is not clear, but the possibility does provide an explanation. Carlile and his wife retired to London, where he died in 1675. He was buried in Petersham churchyard, as was his wife, who survived him by four years. James Carlile was appointed 'sergeant of the hounds of his Royal Highness the Duke of York', presumably when the family left the park.[2]

Sir Daniel Harvey was to become directly involved in the affairs of the park sooner than he must have anticipated when he failed in his attempt to be appointed Ranger. On 19 July 1661 he and Ralph Montagu (probably his brother-in-law, who was later to become the first Duke of Montagu) were jointly awarded the keepership of Hartleton Lodge and Walk, in place of Rogers.[8] The vacancy left by the resignation of Carlile was filled by Colonel Thomas Panton and Bernard Grenville.[9]

Sir Daniel was not to remain in office for long, at least actively, because in December 1667 he was appointed Ambassador to the Ottoman Empire by Charles II,[10] probably because of the Harvey family's strong trading associations with Turkey. He set sail for Turkey in HMS *Leopard* on 18 August 1668,[11] but the ship was delayed in Plymouth, and then at Portland, by storms.[12] It may have been during those delays that he penned a report to the King about the park, the first indication that all was perhaps not under proper control. 'In the Park under my charge which is the best park that is left, for restoring and preserving the deer etc; no groom or huntsman should be allowed a key, as they steal the fawns, nor should the sergeants of the buckhounds have access when his Majesty is not there as they kill the deer, instead of training the hounds.'[13]

The phrase 'the Park under my charge' suggests that Sir Daniel then had custody of the park, but in what capacity is not clear. Sir Lionel Tollemache died at about that time, so it is possible that he may have been Ranger, although he had been promised the custody of the park after Sir Lionel *and* the Countess of Dysart, who was still very much alive and well. In the event, Sir Daniel's departure for Turkey marked the end of his direct association with Richmond Park, for he died in that country, in 1672, without returning to England. However, the family association with the park continued. His wife Elizabeth, Lady Harvey, succeeded him as keeper of Hartleton Lodge and Walk and was still in office in January 1669, because she and Colonel Panton were paid £100 during that month for supplying hay for the deer herds.[14]

All was not well with the deer herds. Treasury papers of 12 October 1669 record that, 'The King says that in the year 1660 there were 2000 deer in Richmond Park and now not above 600 of all sorts and asks the Attorney General which way to [put] out the keepers [whether] by a quo warrant or inquisition.'[15] The Attorney General decided on the latter course, and a hearing was arranged for 25 October 1669. Colonel Panton was called, together with a Captain Coop acting on behalf of Lady Harvey, and explained that he himself had killed about ten deer (he would doubtless have had entitlement to a certain number of deer each year as part of his emoluments), that five hundred had died in one year and that 'the King took away 200'. Other keepers from the park were also called and admitted that about thirty brace of bucks were killed in 1668.[16] It seems that no conclusions were reached as a result of the investigation, and two years later a commission of 'nine gentlemen under the Great Seal' was appointed to enquire into 'the abuses of New Park'.[17] Unfortunately, there is no record of the findings of the Commission, and the severity of the alleged abuses can only be a matter for speculation.

That there had been some abuse there is no doubt. Poaching was not unknown, and in December 1633 George Layton and Enoch Wicklox were indicted for deer stealing in Richmond Park, the informer being none other than Sir Daniel Harvey.[18] Hogs were being illegally brought into the park, to feed on beech mast and acorns at the expense of the deer, and the keepers were instructed to put a stop to the practice. One unnamed keeper was so diligent in doing so, in 1667, that he became involved in an argument with the owner of a herd of hogs, the outcome of which was a broken leg for the owner! The unfortunate keeper duly appeared in front of Bailiff Young at Kingston and was bound over to keep the peace.[19] And there was Sir Daniel's adverse report to the King in 1668.

There are, however, logical explanations which could account for the dramatic drop in the number of deer between 1660 and 1669. The King had indeed instructed that a large number of deer be removed from the park. In 1664 a warrant was issued to Robert Child and William Bowles, Masters of the Toils, instructing them to remove all the red deer (there is no record of this particular aspect of the warrant having been executed), and a hundred brace of fallow deer 'to such places as shall be ordered'.[20] The thirty brace of bucks which the keepers admitted to killing in 1668 were almost certainly animals which had been killed under the authority of a royal warrant, some perhaps destined for the royal table and others for distribution to the officers of the City of London or other favoured persons (see Chapter 3). In earlier centuries large-scale losses in deer herds were not uncommon, the usual cause being disease. Specific diseases were then not recognized as such, and the term 'murrain' was used to describe a whole range of disorders, including anthrax and rabies, affecting animals and domestic stock. In Clarendon Forest 2,209 deer are reputed to have been killed by 'murrain' in 1470, Melksham and Pewsham Forests suffered the loss, by 'murrain', of 340 fallow deer in 1486,[21] and as recently as 1886–7 over 200 fallow died from rabies in Richmond Park.

From the limited evidence available, it seems likely that the fabric of the park had been well cared for during this period. In 1668 £2,000 was spent on the repair of the boundary walls, gates and lodges by the Surveyor General of Works, Sir John Denham.[22] Later the same year he was authorized 'to make bricks in the Great Park at Richmond and to cut furze and ferns there for burning same'.[23] (Bricks thus manufactured from local materials were probably of inferior quality, and this could account for the fact that the oldest sections of the boundary wall today are unlikely to be much more than two hundred years old.) 'The abuses of New Park' between 1660 and 1669 do not appear to have been particularly severe.

It may be that Sir Daniel Harvey had been appointed Ranger before he left for Turkey and retained that office until his death in 1672. Alternatively, the Countess of Dysart may have soldiered on as Ranger after the death of her first husband, with whom she had shared the office since 1660. There is no doubt as to the situation from 8 May 1673 though, for on that date John Maitland, the first Duke of Lauderdale, was appointed sole Ranger of the park.[24] There is more than a hint of intrigue associated with this appointment, because in 1672 he had married his mistress – who was none other than Elizabeth, Countess of Dysart! Maitland was probably at Richmond only infrequently during his tenure as Ranger (1673–83), as he was heavily involved with the affairs of Scotland. Sir Walter Scott described him as a big man with shaggy red hair and coarse features, but with 'a great portion of sense, learning and wit'. Of Lady Dysart he wrote that she was a 'woman of considerable talent, but of inordinate ambition, boundless expense, and the most unscrupulous rapacity'.[25] The King was no doubt only too well aware of her character and ambition because, although she had been granted the right of survivorship to the office of Ranger in 1660, and may have acted as Ranger between 1668 and 1673, she was not confirmed as joint Ranger with her second husband.

Shortly after he became Ranger, Lauderdale brought in two of his servants, John Somervile and Thomas Burford, 'to take care of the deer in New Park, near Richmond'. Their duties and conditions of service are described in the royal warrant which confirmed their appointment in July 1673: 'The Duke of Lauderdale, keeper of said park [New Park], informs me that divers persons unknown, without right, put into said park, horses, cows and other cattle to the prejudice of the feed of the deer, and do other trespasses there, whereby the game will be totally destroyed. You are to provide against all such, and to have keys of all the gates so as to afford you free ingress and regress, and that you may have a convenient abiding place in the park you may inhabit a brick building lately erected on a hill in said park, near the village of Ham, and you may erect such lodges, huts or booths in such places in said park as you shall judge fitting until further order of the King herein, reporting the names of all tresspassers etc. to me.'[26] 'The hill near the village of Ham' is that on which Thatched House Lodge now stands, and the brick building was probably on, or adjacent to, the site of this lodge.

Somervile and Burford were, in effect, working keepers, predecessors of the head and under keepers of the eighteenth and nineteenth centuries. The office of Keeper of a Lodge and Walk fell into disuse a few years later, and Colonel Panton was probably the last of the line. In 1679 he was still resident in the park and was described as one of the head keepers of 'New Park', a position which he may well have retained until his death in 1684 or 1685. The office was replaced by that of the Deputy Ranger, but only after a gap of more than forty years.[27]

After the King had enquired into the reduced strength of the deer herds in 1669, attempts were made to increase their number. In February 1671 a payment of £350 was authorized, in favour of a Mr Baker, for the provision of good upland hay at 35 shillings a load 'for 2500 deer [to be kept] in New Park Co. Surrey'.[28] Here was a declared intent. On 17 November 1676 the Master of the Toils was instructed to 'remove the toils to Hyde Park and take thence 150 deer and carry them to Greenwich Park and the Great Park at Windsor and from thence to the Little Park at Windsor and take from thence 60 deer and carry them also to Windsor Great Park or as he shall receive further directions and from thence to Albury Park near Guildford belonging to the Earl of Warwick and there take 200 deer and carry them to Richmond Park there to be disposed of as

Thomas Delmahoy shall appoint who has presented them to the King'.[29]

According to an entry in Treasury Books of May 1680, 'The hay that was mowed in the meads starved all the deer that winter [1678], and will do so again for the ground is one-third overgrown with rishes this spring ... the meadows in the park will never be good for hay except they be scoured, the bushes grubbed up, the mole hills cut and the trenches cleared'.[30] In June of the same year the grass in the paddocks was considered to be of inferior quality 'and not fit for food for the deer'. The poor-quality grass was cut and sold, and the revenue used to buy good hay for the deer.[31]

The number of deer recorded as having died during the winter of 1678 was six hundred fallow and seven brace of red.[30] Since there is no evidence to the contrary, it has to be assumed that, despite this heavy loss, a sufficient number of both fallow and red deer survived to maintain the viability of the herds. This, in turn, suggests that the number of deer in the park prior to the winter of 1678 was substantially higher than in 1669, although it is not clear if the target figure of 2,500 was reached. What is clear is that the condition of the park was deteriorating.

The Duke of Lauderdale died in 1683, and despite his widow's right of survivorship (granted in 1660), Charles II appointed Laurence Hyde, first Earl of Rochester and second son of the great Earl of Clarendon, Ranger of Richmond Park. Hyde's sister Anne was married to the Duke of York, later to be James II, and this may well have influenced the King's decision to favour him at the expense of The Countess of Dysart. The office then attracted a salary of 6 shillings a day, an entitlement to three bucks and three does in due season each year (fee deer), and certain other perquisites, including the right to graze cattle and pigs in the park, providing that this did not conflict with the interests of the deer.[32]

The appointment of a new Ranger did nothing to prevent the clouds of neglect gathering. In 1685 the Earl of Rochester was required to 'cause such convenient parts in said park [Richmond Park] as are overgrown and run with moss, weeds, furze or rushes to be forthwith ploughed and sown with corn for two or three years next ensuing and to be well dunged the last year and laid down very smooth and level as well for the meliorating the feed of the said ground for the benefit of the deer, as for the better riding and evener going thereon; the King being informed that several parts of the meadow and other grounds there are so overrun with moss etc. and that the best way to kill same is by ploughing'.[33] There is no record as to whether or not those agricultural operations were carried out.

James II (1685–8), that unfortunate monarch whose reign was to be so brief, granted the lease of Petersham Lodge to the Earl of Rochester (the lease was in fact held by Edward Hyde as Lord Cornbury, and Charles Boyle as trustees for the Earl) in 1686. Twelve years later, a further grant of thirty-nine acres of parkland was added to the property.[34]

James II probably did not hunt in the park, but William of Orange (William III, 1689–1702), regularly used Richmond Park as a hunting ground, although he was more interested in shooting than hunting with hounds. On 30 November 1697, 'The King went to Richmond on Saturday and took the diversion of shooting. The pain he had in his knee is over.'[35] And on 4 February 1698, 'The King is gone to Richmond to shoot, and stays there all night.'[36] In April 1696 Sir William Parkyns and Sir John Friend were executed after being found guilty of conspiring to murder the King on his return journey from a hunting expedition in the park to Kensington Palace.[37]

The King occasionally hunted from horseback too, and his death at the comparatively early age of fifty-one is attributed by some to an injury received as a result of a fall from his horse while hunting in Richmond Park.[38] But drama and tragedy were by no means regular companions of the King on hunting days. His Yeoman of the Field enjoyed an issue of two manchets (a bread made from fine wheat), two bottles of Lambeth ale, two of champagne, two of rhenish (Rhine wine) and two of Spanish (presumably sherry) when in attendance. The Yeoman of the Field to the Queen (Mary II, 1689–96) received the same when she was present. Hunting days could be merry occasions![39]

A keeper by the name of 'Aldridg' is first mentioned in Treasury Books of 1699.[40] In 1714 a record of wages paid to park staff for the half year shows that 'Waldritch' (presumably Aldridg), a keeper, earned £12. 10s. 0d. Theophilus Westwood, another keeper, £10, Henry Badger, molecatcher, £7, and the Park Bailiff £5.[41] Two years later £40 was spent on the repair of Aldridge's Lodge, which stood on the site of Thatched House Lodge.[42] In earlier centuries it was common practice to name lodges after the occupant, particularly if they were senior members of staff, and Aldridge's Lodge continued to be called by that name at least until 1754.[43] According to one source, 'Theophilus' Aldridge was one of four keepers, whose duties included 'watching, keeping and preserving the game of all kinds within and for the district of 10 miles about the Palaces of Richmond and Hampton Court' in 1733. (Another was William Lowen, about whom more of later.) Their annual salary was £30 and they also received an annual allowance to purchase and maintain their livery.[44] It seems probable that 'Theophilus Aldridg' was one of the Richmond Park keepers. He may have been the 'Waldritch' who was paid £12. 10s. 0d. for a half year in 1714, and he could conceivably have been the head keeper of the day, in view of the £2. 10s. 0d salary advantage he enjoyed over 'Theophilus' Westwood.

The name Aldridge was associated with the park for the minimum period of 1699 to 1754. It was by no means uncommon for son to follow in

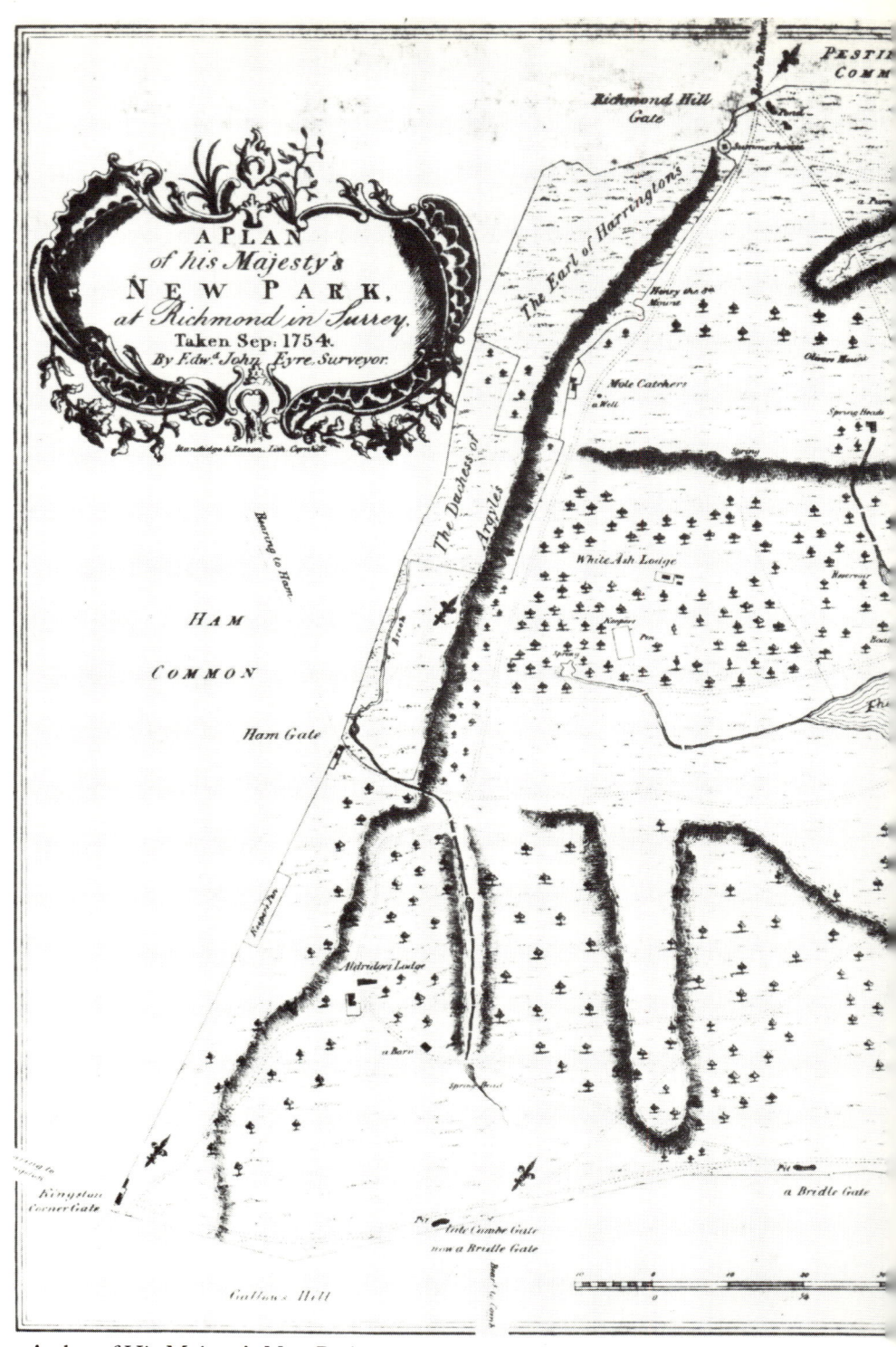

A plan of His Majesty's New Park made in 1754, surveyor, John Eyre

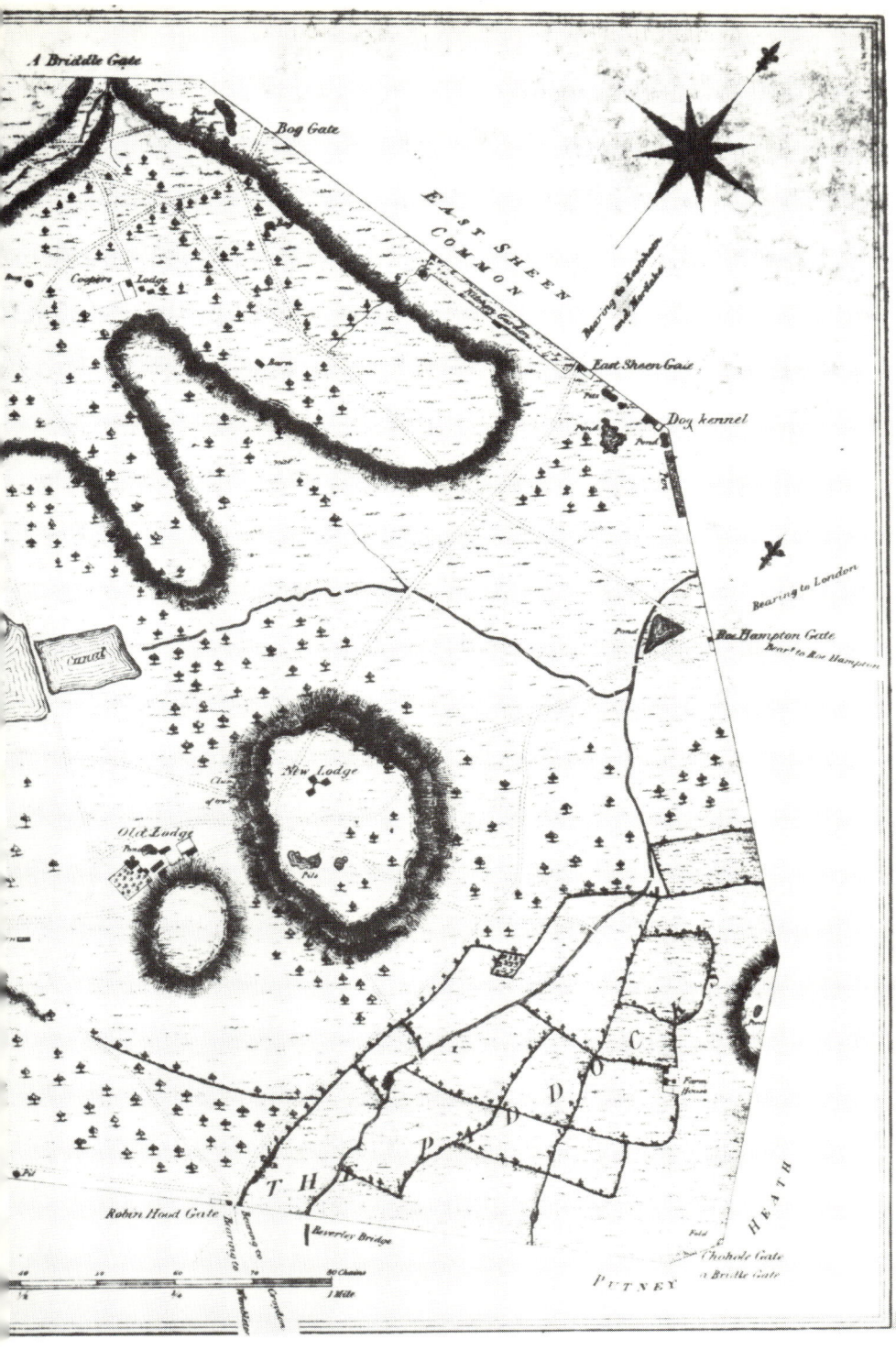

A Briddle Gate

Bog Gate

EAST SHEEN COMMON

Coopers Lodge

Barn

East Sheen Gate

Dog kennel

Pond Pond

Pond

Bearing to London

Canal

Pond Roe Hampton Gate
Bears to Roe Hampton

New Lodge

Old Lodge

Pits

Farm House

C

D O

P D

T H E

Robin Hood Gate

Beverley Bridge

HEATH

Field

Thatchde Gate
a Briddle Gate

PUTNEY

50 Chains

1 Mile

father's footsteps at that time, and it is likely that more than one generation of the family served in the park as keepers. Evidence to support this is to be found today in Petersham churchyard, where the grave of one Charles Aldridge, who died in 1736 at the age of fifty-nine, is close to those of other keepers who served in Richmond Park.

On the death of Laurence, Earl of Rochester, in 1711, his son Henry Hyde, Earl of Clarendon and second Earl of Rochester, was appointed Ranger, in accordance with the command of Queen Anne (1702–14), who in the year of her accession, granted Laurence Hyde the rangership of the park for a further two generations.[45] The Queen agreed to the office being sub-granted to Francis Gwyn and Richard Powys,[46] and Henry Hyde seems to have played little part in the affairs of the park. He did, however, prevent eighty oaks being felled for the completion of a chapel of ease beside the parish church on Kew Green,[47] and in June 1716 he petitioned the King concerning the condition of the park. According to the Earl, 'The Great Lodge [Petersham Lodge] in Richmond Great Park, the wall and the ponds in the said Park and several other places are very ruinous and decayed condition . . .'.[48] That his petition was successful, at least to some degree, is evident from a warrant issued later that year to Edward Young, Surveyor General of Woods, detailing the cost of repairs to walls, gates etc., Aldridge's Lodge, the Great Pond Head and drains 'being about 16 miles'.[42]

During the period reviewed in this chapter, there is little doubt that the condition of the park had deteriorated to some extent. But effort had also been made to combat the worst of the neglect and abuse. The rights of access which Charles I had been obliged to concede when gathering together the various areas of land which went to make up his New Park in 1637 remained unaffected. Charles II, in 1671, paid out £30 'as our promise to the poor for preventing their destroying the woods in the said park [New Park] according to an agreement of our late royal father upon taking in the commons'.[28] William III and Mary II are reputed to have made public access to the park much easier, although by today's standards it was still very restricted. Between 1673 and 1683 there was considerable gravel extraction, and as many as eight thousand loads were dug.[49] This was probably controlled extraction, however, and it is not impossible that the shape and area of the Pen Ponds, as they are today, were determined by those excavations. The fortunes of the deer herds waxed and waned, but there is nothing to suggest that there were not viable herds of both red and fallow in the park at the end of this period. Horace Walpole, writing about Richmond Park as it was at the close of the Hyde rangerships in 1727, described it as 'a bog and a harbour for deer-stealers and vagabonds'.[50] The judgement seems rather harsh. The basic character of the park remained secure, although it may have been a little dented.

6

The Park – to the End of the Eighteenth Century

George II (1727–60), in the year of his accession, appointed Robert, Lord Walpole, as Ranger, but he seems to have occupied the office only nominally, granting most of the rights and perquisites attached to it to his father, Sir Robert Walpole, the Prime Minister. Sir Robert became, in all but name, the Ranger. It was during this period that Richmond Park reached its peak as a hunting ground, and Sir Robert was closely associated with this activity. Such was his interest that, during the week, when he was in London, he was reputed to open and read any letters from his gamekeepers before attending to official business. And it is said that the closing of the House of Commons on Saturdays dates from this time, in order that the Prime Minister could attend the Saturday meets of the Royal Buckhounds!

Hunting was well organized, and the King, the Court and Sir Robert Walpole hunted regularly during the season. George II had hunted at Richmond while still Prince of Wales, as in 1725 Lady Mary Wortley Montagu mentioned in a letter to her sister, the Countess of Mar: 'I spend many hours on horseback, and I'll assure you, ride stag hunting, which I know you'll stare to hear of. I have arrived to vast courage and skill that way, and am so well pleased with it as with the acquisition of a new sense. His Royal Highness [the Prince of Wales] hunts in Richmond Park, and I make one of the "*beau mond*" in his train.'[1]

A picture of a royal hunt during the reign of George II can be drawn from a report which was published in the *Stamford Mercury* (and also in *Read's Journal*) in August 1728: 'On Saturday their Majesties together with their Royal Highnesses the Duke [of Cumberland] and the Princesses, came to the New Park by Richmond from Hampton Court and diverted themselves with hunting a stag, which ran from eleven to one, when he took to the great pond, where he defended himself for half an hour, when he was killed. His Majesty, the Duke, and the Princess Royal

71

Sir Robert Walpole in Richmond Park, by Robert Wootton

hunted on horseback, her Majesty and the Princess Amelia in a four wheeled chaise, Princess Caroline in a two-wheeled chaise, and the Princesses Mary and Louisa in a coach. Sir Robert attended as Ranger, clothed in green.'[2]

Henrietta, Countess of Suffolk, wrote on 31 July 1730; 'We hunt here [Richmond Park] with great noise and violence, and have everyday a tolerable chance to have a neck broke.'[3] This seems to have been no exaggeration, and there are accounts of Princess Amelia being thrown from her horse when a stag turned on it 'and due to her Petticoat hanging on the Pommel of the Saddle' dragged for some distance before being rescued.[4] In August 1731 the Hon. Mr Fitzwilliam, Page of Honour to His Majesty, and his horse came to grief 'among the coney-burrows' (rabbit burrows). Three days later, a chaise overturned, fortunately without injury to driver and passenger, and one of the King's huntsmen, a Mr Shuter, had a fall from his horse and received a slight contusion on his head. The following month Sir Robert Walpole was thrown from his horse 'but he received no injury, yet her Majesty ordered him to be bled by way of precaution'.[5]

In 1732 the Royal Buckhounds met on no fewer than thirteen occasions in Richmond Park, the opening meet being on 22 July and the final meet on 15 November. In other years a lesser number were staged in the park, but meets were also arranged in other venues not far away. Windsor Forest was a popular choice, as was Hounslow Heath; Sunbury Common was also hunted from time to time.[6] In April 1706 there is record of the 'Queen's Buckhounds' meeting on Putney Heath, the quarry being fallow buck on that occasion.[7] Here is explanation for certain of the park's keepers' having jurisdiction for ten miles around the park, as well as their responsibilities within the park. Here is also a hint that there were feral herds of deer on those heaths and commons, for the practice of 'enlarging' (setting free) captive deer from carts, brought to the site of a meet for hunting, does not seem to have been established until the middle of the eighteenth century.

It was during this period that the first signs of restraint on public access to the park became apparent. There were several reasons for the introduction of restrictions, mainly, but probably not exclusively, associated with the deer herds and hunting. The venue for the opening meet of the Royal Buckhounds, on 9 August 1735, was Richmond Park. Some time prior to the opening date it was announced that, 'Upon account of the great Crowds and Throngs of People that have attended the Stag Hunting at New-Park, when the Royal Family were hunting there, which has Rendered the Riding there not only troublesome, but very dangerous, her Majesty has been pleased to order, That no Person shall be admitted into the Park without a Hunting Ticket, prepared for that Purpose, with the

Date of the Day, and the Seal of the Ranger; to be given Weekly, by the Ranger or his Deputy, upon proper Application.'[8] The following year a Mr Lowther was instructed to 'pay out of the King's money in his hands £892-5-0d. for "Daily Gazetters" sent to the Post Office between 1736, March 30, and June 29 following, as also £1-17-6d. for notices in the public papers that no persons could hunt in Richmond Park without hunting tickets'.[9]

The 'fence month' was a procedure whereby the grazing of domestic stock in the royal forests was prohibited for the two weeks prior to, and the two weeks after, Midsummer Day. The origins of the custom date back to the medieval period, the intention being to keep disturbance to a minimum during the time when calves and fawns were at their most vulnerable, and also to conserve natural food supplies so that those would be more readily available to lactating hinds and does. Observation of the fence month was probably extended to parks at an early date, although there is no reference to its operating in Richmond Park until early in the eighteenth century, at which time it was extended to an eight-week period; as one contemporary author put it: '. . . not long afterwards fence-month was invented, which was clapping May and June together and calling it fence-month'.[10] No specific date is recorded for the introduction of the extended fence month, but it was probably early in the reign of George II.

It has been suggested that Sir Robert Walpole was anxious to curtail public access to the park for more personal reasons too, and he seems to have come to regard it more as a private estate than a park. He is reputed to have had removed some of the ladder stiles which were set up against the boundary wall at various points to provide access for the ordinary person, and also to have built lodges for gate-keepers at some of the gates, so that access by equestrian traffic and carriages could be controlled more effectively.[11] The only survivor of the original gate lodges, built in 1742, is at Ham Gate. Sir Robert's stamp on the development of Richmond Park is neatly summed up in the *Victoria County Histories*, Surrey edition: 'The Prime Minister, although he effected improvements and spent much money on the Park, made several infringments on the rights of the public by shutting up gates and taking away stepladders on the walls.'

One of the buildings on which Sir Robert spent a considerable sum of money was Hartleton Lodge. He enlarged the building by the addition of two wings, and, according to an eighteenth-century engraving, it was a grand and imposing building with a landscaped pond adjacent. A few hundred yards away, to the south, another building was in the course of construction, a hunting lodge for the royal family. This was Stone Lodge, whose name was soon changed to New Lodge to identify it from Old Lodge, by which name Hartleton Lodge had by then become known.[12] In

Old Lodge and Stone Lodge (now White Lodge) in the eighteenth century

White Lodge from Queen's Ride

due course the new building was to be renamed White Lodge, the name by which it is known today. £500 was spent in making a road to the lodge, fitting out the kitchen 'and making a straight joint floor and Portland chimney-piece to the great room' in 1729.[13] This was the central section of the lodge, constructed of Portland stone; the two brick-built wings were added some twenty-five years later.

On 9 June 1736 the Surveyor General of Woods was authorized to spend £600 for making new roads 'for the convenience of the Royal Family in their passage from the Royal Gardens at Kew to and through Richmond New Park'.[14] At about the same time a private entrance for the royal family was constructed on the northern boundary of the park, leading from Sheen Common. This access was originally known as Queen's Gate, but it was later changed to Bog Gate, on account of the marshy ground immediately within the entrance.[15] Queen's Ride, a broad, tree-lined avenue leading away from the west elevation of White Lodge, first comes to notice on Rocque's *Survey of London*, published in 1746[16] and was named as such after Queen Caroline, wife of George II. The *Survey* gives the impression that the woods on either side of the Ride were mature, which suggests that the avenue may have been hewn out of existing woodland, perhaps in 1736, or the following year, to complete the route between the royal residence at Kew and the King's new hunting lodge in the park. Another lodge which dates from about this time is Bog Lodge, in the north of the park, which is shown as Cooper's Lodge on Rocque's *Survey* and on Eyre's plan of 1754.[17] Bog Lodge was, for many years, the residence of the head keeper, and it is likely that it was originally built for this purpose. Also shown on Rocque's *Survey* is a small unnamed building on the park boundary wall, a few hundred yards to the east of Sheen Gate; by 1754 this was known as 'the Dog Kennel'. In October 1733 Sir Robert promoted William Lowen, Yeoman-Pricker (marker of the hounds' feet) of the Royal Buckhounds, to 'Huntsman of the Harriers [hare and/or fox hounds] in the New Park near Richmond',[18] and both huntsman and hounds may well have been occupied this building. Not shown on the *Survey*, but well established by 1754, was White Ash Lodge, the traditional residence of the second keeper, with a 'keepers' pen' nearby.

A second tree-lined avenue is shown on the Rocque *Survey*, leading eastward from King Henry VIII Mound – about which more in a later chapter.

The office of Deputy Ranger was created in the 1730s, probably to take over the responsibilities of the day-to-day management and administration of the park, which were becoming increasingly complex. On 21 June 1733 'Captain Edward Jackson, deputy ranger of Richmond New Park' successfully petitioned the Surveyor General of Woods for £922.

12s. 8¾d. to pay for 'works and repairs' in the park.[19] In this instance the money was found from the proceeds of wood sales from the park; three years later there is another reference to wood sales being used to 'defray cost of works . . . in Richmond Park'.[20] It seems likely that the increasing costs of maintaining the park were financed by the sale of wood and other produce, as well as from the revenues of Crown lands[21] and other sources.

The grave of Joseph Cooper, 'late keeper of Richmond Park', who died on 7 February 1735, is in Petersham churchyard, as is that of his son Augustine, who died on 3 July 1775, aged sixty-three. This was probably the family who occupied Cooper's Lodge — now Bog Lodge — and it is likely that Augustine Cooper was the head keeper of his day — as was perhaps his father before him, because it was then not uncommon for several members of one family to follow the same trade or profession, and for son to follow in father's footsteps. Thus William Lowen, Huntsman of the Harriers in Richmond Park, may well have been related to a William Lowen, who was described as a 'chief huntsman' in 1712,[22] and George Lowan, Chief Huntsman to the King in 1742.[23]

There is an interesting story concerning a 'black' (blackamoor) by the name of Cato, who was reputed 'to blow the best French Horn and Trumpet in England'. Cato, it is said, was once in the service of Sir Robert Walpole but in or about 1733 was given as a gift to the Prince and Princess of Wales by the Earl of Chesterfield. The Prince of Wales appointed Cato head gamekeeper at 'Cliefden', and afterwards at Richmond Park.[24] There is no mention of Cato in official records, and it is unlikely that he was employed in the park in an official capacity although he may have been retained by Sir Robert Walpole as a personal gamekeeper.

Of the remainder of the staff in Richmond Park during this period there is little record. One post which would doubtless have been occupied was that of mole-catcher, and on Rocque's *Survey* a building is shown, on or near the site of Pembroke Lodge, which was later described as the mole-catcher's lodge. Another post which was unlikely to have been vacant, in view of the considerable amount of work going on in the park, was that of bailiff. A keeper by the name of Lucas was recruited, early in the eighteenth century, from the Duke of Newcastle's estate at Claremont, near Esher. His main attribute appears to have been his skill in fighting with the quarterstaff (a stout wooden pole used as a weapon of defence), a useful skill to have when dealing with poachers.[25] Lucas was probably employed in a relatively junior capacity, but his appointment is worthy of note since he was the first of a family which was to be closely involved with the affairs of the park for the next 150 years.

In the absence of detailed records, it can only be assumed that the deer herds were in satisfactory condition during the earlier years of the eighteenth century. Indeed they must have been, in view of the popularity of the park as a royal hunting ground. In 1732 one Charles Howard was paid £87 for catching up and transporting red deer from Horton, Northamptonshire, to 'Richmond New Park'.[26] Two years later deer (probably red) were brought to the park from the Earl of Salisbury's woods at Hoddesdon, Hertfordshire.[27] There were outgoings too. In 1742 George Lowan, Chief Huntsman to the King, was paid £78 for taking red deer to Epping Forest.[23] The following year he received £128 for catching up red deer and transporting them to Windsor Forest.[28] The stock of deer is unlikely to have been particularly large; too many could well have interfered with the hunting. The introductions of red deer recorded above may have been designed to improve the quality of the red deer by bringing in 'new blood', and the deer removed to Epping and Windsor to reduce the herd size to manageable proportions *vis-à-vis* hunting.

Sir Robert Walpole died in 1745, and his son, Lord Walpole, six years later. Deer hunting in the park seems to have come to an end with the demise of the Walpoles, and the Royal Buckhounds made their last visit to Richmond Park in 1753.[29] This was, however, not to be the end of the park's association with deer hunting, as will be explained in later chapters.

On the death of Lord Walpole, the King appointed his youngest daughter, Princess Amelia, Ranger. It is not altogether clear whether she resided at Old Lodge or White Lodge during her period as Ranger; accounts differ. The fact that construction of the brick-built wings at White Lodge was not completed until 1761,[30] which year marked the end of Princess Amelia's tenure, suggests that she may have spent her years in the Park at Old Lodge.

Shortly after taking up her appointment, she completed the process which Sir Robert Walpole had started – she denied access to the park to all but her friends. There was considerable protest as a result, culminating in an attempt by a Richmond brewer, John Lewis, to obtain a court judgement against the Ranger's action in excluding the public. He was successful, and the Princess was ordered by the court to replace the ladder stiles in their appointed positions on the boundary walls. She complied but spaced the rungs so wide apart that access was virtually impossible. A further court action ensued, and public access was eventually restored. John Lewis was saddled with considerable legal expenses, however, and his financial position was further exacerbated by the flooding of his business premises beside the Thames. He died in poverty in 1792.[31]

Princess Amelia's behaviour did not make her the most popular of Rangers, and, shortly after the death of her father in 1760, she surrendered the rangership. She is reputed to have been responsible for the formation of the Pen Ponds, but this seems most unlikely since Rocque's *Survey* of 1746 depicts the ponds much as they are today. And she herself

Right: Plan of Richmond Park made for Princess Amelia in 1754 (J. Eyre, Surveyor)

was hunting (in a four-wheel chaise) on that day in 1728 when a stag was killed in 'the great pond' – presumably the Upper Pen Pond.

Although George III (1760–1820) appointed John Stuart, third Earl of Bute, as Ranger in 1761, the King was not content to leave the management and administration of the park entirely to him. George took an active interest himself, and his involvement is well illustrated by the following text, from Home Office Papers dated 25 June 1761: 'Mr. C. Jenkinson (for the Earl of Bute) to John Pitt Esq. What he has represented as to the nature of his office is true, and it has been usual for the Surveyor of Woods to execute all repairs and works in the Royal Parks. But in the case in question the King, considering Richmond and all the buildings belonging to it as one of his palaces and places of residence, determined that the repairs should be executed under his own eye by the Board of Works who are constantly employed in such cases, and has given directions accordingly.'[32]

Immediately after his appointment, the Earl of Bute arranged for the transfer of the Royal Fox and Harrier Pack from Richmond to Windsor, where they were kept until 1782, when the pack was finally disbanded.[33] George III also instructed that wild turkeys should no longer be raised and kept in the park.[34] The wild turkey, a North American bird brought to England by Turkish traders in 1521, may have been first introduced into the park during the later years of the seventeenth century; William of Orange was reputedly 'a good shot at winged game, preserved pheasants, wild turkeys and "such small deer" at Hampton Court, Windsor, Richmond and other royal manors'.[35] Early in the eighteenth century flocks of up to three thousand were to be found in the park, and they were hunted by using dogs to flush them up into the trees, where they were shot by George II and others. They were large, heavy birds, some of the old cocks weighing as much as 30 lb.[36]

Royal interest and participation in hunting continued during the reign of George III. He is credited with being the first monarch to hunt deer enlarged from a deer cart, and enjoyed the reputation of upholding the highest traditions of the chase. The transfer of the harrier pack, and the decision to discontinue the by then established custom of maintaining wild turkeys for sport, may thus be thought to be out of character. But the King was well aware of the apprehension of the local populace. The loss of access to the park was still fresh in their minds. Public access was eased, and every endeavour was made to allay any suspicion that the restrictions of the past few decades would be re-introduced. The park continued to be used as a hunting ground, but on a much reduced scale. 'Field sports' were confined mainly to game-bird shooting and hare-coursing.

The cessation of deer-hunting reduced the pressures on the deer herds, but the relief was to be short lived. With the continuing disafforestation of the royal forests, those who were responsible for the administration of the Royal Venison Warrant were becoming increasingly reliant on the fallow deer herds of the royal parks for the large quantities of venison required to satisfy the needs of the warrant. As the eighteenth century drew to a close, so the demands on the fallow deer herds of the parks multiplied – so much so that by 1789 the Deputy Ranger, the Hon James Stuart (son of the Ranger), reported that the park was in 'great Want of a Supply of Deer'. £273 was subsequently spent on the purchase of 76½ brace of fallow deer 'for his Majesty's Service'. The transaction involved eight brace of bucks at 5 guineas a brace, 14½ brace of sores at four guineas a brace, 21 brace of prickets at three guineas a brace, and 33 brace of does at the same price.[37] There is also evidence of an importation of red deer from Germany, possibly in the early years of the reign of George III, because on 10 January 1790 W. Harris, a gardener at Thatched House Lodge, shot an old stag, 'the only one left that came from Hanover'.[38]

The salaries and emoluments of the park staff in the later years of the eighteenth century are not well documented, but one record, dated 1788, shows that the Ranger was paid a salary of £109. 10s. 0d. a year, the head keeper £69, the first underkeeper £20 and the second £25. This was by no means the keepers' only source of income, for they had entitlement to certain fees and other payments. The first underkeeper's income from those sources was presumably greater than that of the second; hence the disparity in their salaries. A mole-catcher was still employed, receiving an annual salary of £14. The bailiff received £10 a year.[39] All, with the possible exception of the bailiff, lived in the park rent free and enjoyed perquisites such as an allowance of firewood, and the right to graze a specified number of cattle. On 1 June 1806 there were eighty-nine cows and oxen at large in the park, the property of the Ranger and staff.[40]

Two major factors mark eighteenth-century Richmond Park. The middle of the century saw the end of an era, that of deer hunting, the second half the establishment of a new era, that of large-scale venison production. The second factor involved the loss of the right of public access in a manner which can only be described as autocratic. However, by the end of the century the right of public access had been re-established, more firmly than ever. There were other developments too. Building activity was considerable, ranging from the provision of staff lodges to the more magnificent White Lodge, a hunting retreat for royalty. A hint, but no more, of formality was introduced by way of Queen's Ride and the short, tree-lined avenue leading eastward from Henry VIII Mound. But, at the close of the century the fundamental medieval flavour and character of the park remained intact.

7

The Park – the Early Nineteenth Century

On the death of the Earl of Bute in 1792, George III took the rangership of Richmond Park into his own hands, the first monarch to do so. He had ambitious plans for developing the park, involving extensive land drainage, tree-planting schemes and even a certain amount of arable cultivation,[1] the latter possibly with the intention of making the park self-sufficient in winter feed for the deer herds, game birds and other livestock. In the event, the King's ambitions were not fully realized, probably because of the deterioration of his health in his later years, and the pressures exerted by affairs of state.

Some tree-planting was, however, carried out, particularly along the north boundary between Richmond and Roehampton Gates and, in the south, between Robin Hood and Kingston Gates.[2] It is possible that 'Capability' Brown (1715–83), whose work had such a profound influence on the English landscape, may have been associated with those early tree-planting schemes. Brown was appointed Surveyor to His Majesty's Gardens and Waters in 1764 and was based at Hampton Court. He was reputedly responsible for superintending the planting of a group of elms on the slight ridge which runs east to west on the north-east of Barn Wood, near to Bog Lodge. (A group of mature elm trees in this location was felled in the late 1970s, having been struck down with Dutch Elm Disease. Their age was assessed at just over one hundred years, and they could, therefore, have been planted in succession to Brown's elms, although there are no records to substantiate this.) George III is also credited with altering the line of the road running eastward from Richmond Gate to its present line, at the beginning of the nineteenth century. A contemporary account describes it thus: '. . . and a very beautiful drive it is, having the appearance of a Royal Domain. There are some fine timber trees in this line of road . . .'[3]

As to the King's agricultural intentions, little seems to have come of

Richmond Gate from Richmond Hill in 1798

them. Attempts were made to grow cereals, but they proved unsuccessful because of the poor nutrimental value of the soil, and deer damage to the growing crops.[4]

Pembroke Lodge, the mole-catcher's lodge of earlier date, was developed towards the end of the eighteenth century by the architect Sir John Soane, for the Countess of Pembroke. The lodge had been occupied by a gamekeeper called Trage, a member of George II's household. The Countess, a prominent lady at the Court of George III, successfully persuaded the King to grant her the lease, and by the time of her death there in 1831 (aged ninety-four), the building had assumed its present form. A new lodge was built for Trage near Richmond Gate, but this was demolished some time afterwards – it is said on account of its ugliness.[5] George III was also responsible for the construction of Richmond Gate

83

Pembroke Lodge in the nineteenth century

Left: Richmond Gate today with the Gate Lodge, built in 1798

and Lodge in 1798 (to replace the then existing gates, for Richmond Gate was one of the six original gates into the park.) The design has been attributed to 'Capability' Brown, but it is more likely that the gates and lodge were the work of Sir John Soane, who was by then the Deputy Surveyor of HM Woods and Forests.[6]

A gamekeeper's lodge, later to be known as Ladderstile Gate Lodge, was built at the Coombe entrance to the park, on the south boundary, in the 1780s. A twin-gabled building, it was equipped with a stable for the occupant's working horse, a cowshed for the cows which he was entitled to keep by virtue of his job, and a large compound for grazing domestic stock. It was at this entrance that the last of the ladder stiles, which afforded pedestrian access to the park in place of gates, was replaced by a pedestrian gate in 1884–5.[7] The name of this lodge, and the gate, commemorates not only the end of a means of access which was as old as the park but the successful preservation of the right of public access to Richmond Park, granted by Charles I in 1637. The present iron cradle gates were erected in 1901.

An account relating to the construction of a cesspool, and for walling the cellar of the lodge, in 1787, also refers to the rebuilding of sections of the boundary wall between Ham and Kingston Gates, near Roehampton Gate, and at 'Coombe Ladderstile'. The new bricks used for the work are described as 'Gray Stocks', and there is mention of 'cleaning old bricks' for re-use.[8] It is doubtful if, by this time, any of the original wall still survived, and even the bricks cleaned for re-use are unlikely to have been the original bricks, which were made from local materials and manufactured on site.

By 1771 Cooper's Lodge had become Lucas's Lodge,[9] and there is little doubt that by then a Lucas, possibly the son of the Lucas recruited during the reign of George I, was head keeper. In the latter part of the eighteenth century one Samuel Hayes was first under keeper and, as such, resident at White Ash Lodge. In 1787 he employed a young man by the name of James Sawyer, who had been recommended to The Deputy Ranger, the Hon James Stuart, by the Marquis of Lothian. Sawyer came from a long line of deer- and park-keepers and, although he had been articled to a Norfolk land agent and steward, expressed a keen desire to follow in his father's profession, his father being head keeper to the Duke of Rutland at Clevely.[3] James Sawyer was the first member of a second family whose professional association with Richmond Park was to last well over a hundred years.

Within a few years Sawyer had succeeded Hayes as first under keeper. John Lucas, the head keeper, died in 1795, and Sawyer was promoted to that office in preference to Lucas's son, also named John, who was considered too young to succeed his father.[10] Instead, he filled the vacancy created by Sawyer's elevation. Shortly after moving to the head keeper's lodge, Sawyer married Anne Gooch, of Ham, and their first son, John, was born in 1798. He was eventually to leave the park to farm Ham Manor Farm, near Ham Gate, but his brother James, a year his junior, was destined to follow in his father's footsteps.[11]

In his capacity as Ranger, the King sometimes dealt directly with the head keeper, as is evident from an account of expenses incurred by Sawyer in 1797–8. The account is headed 'His Majesty's Direction to James Sawyer'. It details the costs of catching up an unspecified number of red deer, probably destined for the Royal Hunt headquarters at Swinley, near Ascot, in November 1797. The toils used to catch up the deer required the attendance of seventeen men for two days and were hired for the occasion at a cost of two guineas. A further charge of one guinea was, however, levied for the repair of damage sustained by the toils during the operation. Both Sawyer and Lucas attended on horseback, for which they claimed expenses of one guinea each. The same account refers 'to the expenses of attending the catching of hares in Richmond Park to send to Windsor' (presumably for the royal table) in February 1798, and the cost of 'several times repairing the hare hayes' was nineteen shillings. According to this account, steel vermin traps cost 3s. 7d. each at this time.[12]

During the reign of George III, hunting the carted deer was becoming increasingly popular. The object of this form of hunting, patronized by the Court, was the chase and not the kill, the hounds being trained to leave the quarry unmolested when it was brought 'to bay' (facing and standing up to the hounds). The animal was then recovered and returned to the hunt paddock so that it could be hunted again, and a deer which gave good sport was often hunted several times a season for several seasons. The selected animal was taken to the place of the meet in a specially designed cart (hence the term 'carted deer'), from which it was enlarged. A certain amount of 'law' (the time that elapsed between the deer being released from the cart, and the hounds being 'laid on') was allowed, which varied from five to fifteen minutes, depending on the individual animal, the terrain being hunted over, and other considerations. Red deer were almost exclusively used for this type of hunting.

Richmond Park was one of the several sources of red deer for the Royal Hunt. Sometimes deer which had served the hunt well, and had escaped serious injury, were returned to the park to spend their remaining years in retirement, and possibly in an attempt to build up a stock of deer of good hunting quality. Stags so returned tended to be aggressive and dangerous 'at a particular time of the year' (presumably during the rut), and occasionally the keepers were obliged to fire at them with buckshot to turn away a charge.[13]

One particular stag, which was returned to the park from the Royal Hunt deer paddock, bearing the name 'Sir Edmund', caused no trouble at all, however, and during his years in retirement herded with the cattle in the park, in preference to his own kind. This stag had, on one occasion, given a particularly good account of himself in the hunting field. One of the few riders in at the 'take' (the climax of the hunt) was Sir Edmund Nagle, and the King, who was also in the 'field', was so delighted with the outcome that he decreed that the stag should thereafter be called 'Sir Edmund'. After several years of retirement, 'Sir Edmund' reputedly died, of natural causes, on the same day as Sir Edmund Nagle passed away.[14]

The early years of the nineteenth century brought with them changes in the administrative structure of the royal parks and forests. During the seventeenth and eighteenth centuries, the management of the land revenues of the Crown was the combined responsibility of the Surveyor General of Land Revenues and the Surveyor General of Woods, Forests, Parks and Chases. Although both Surveyors were involved in the affairs of the park to some extent, the Ranger of the park was directly responsible to the monarch, and therefore wielded considerable authority.

On his accession in 1760, George III surrendered to Parliament the revenues from the Crown lands, in return for a fixed Civil List – a procedure still followed today. No doubt as a result of this, Commissioners were appointed, in 1786, to enquire into the state of the woods, forests and land revenues of the Crown.

After considerable deliberation, they eventually recommended that the Crown estates should be managed by a board of three persons, the Commissioners of Woods, Forests and Land Revenues, but it was not until 1810 that the recommendation was executed (Stat. 5 George III c 65). This was the end of the two Surveyor Generals of previous centuries, but a third Surveyor General still retained an interest in the royal parks. He was the Surveyor General of Works and Public Buildings, an office which had developed over the centuries from the builders, carpenters and plumbers who had built and maintained the palaces and other royal residences. Until the 1830s maintenance of the parks and palaces was financed mainly from land revenues and other non-Parliamentary sources, but in 1831 the Surveyor General of Works and Public Buildings was made responsible to Parliament for the ordinary repair and maintenance of most of the royal parks, gardens and palaces. This somewhat cumbersome administrative structure was eased, to some degree, by the Office of Woods, Forests and Land Revenues absorbing that of Works and Public Buildings in 1832 (Stats. 2 & 3 William IV c 2).

During his latter years, George III's association with the park was probably very limited, although the year before he gave up the rangership he made what was to prove a very important appointment. In 1814 the

Viscount Sidmouth, Deputy Ranger of Richmond Park, 1813–44

King was succeeded as Ranger by his daughter Elizabeth, Landgravine of Hesse-Homburg.[15] By then the office had become very much a sinecure, and the active management of the park was largely in the hands of the Board of Commissioners and the Deputy Ranger, to which office George III appointed the politician Henry Addington, Viscount Sidmouth, in 1813. Lord Sidmouth was to have a profound effect on Richmond Park, so much so that the head keeper was moved to record that, 'The deer in Richmond Park had been greatly improved since the term of Deputy Rangership of Viscount Sidmouth and the Park so much that all the neighbourhood were congratulating his Lordship.'[16]

Though not Deputy Ranger until 1813, Lord Sidmouth had lived in White Lodge since the beginning of the century, and he continued to do so until his death in 1844. During his long tenure he was host to many of the eminent men of the day, and his guests included the playwright Sheridan, the novelist Sir Walter Scott, the younger Pitt and Admiral Lord Nelson. Another visitor of note was the landscape gardener Humphrey Repton. Repton used to demonstrate designs to his clients with a drawing of the site, superimposing upon it a slide showing his proposed design. He designed the gardens of White Lodge (little of the original gardens remain), and his plate of the west elevation, as he found it, shows open parkland stretching to the walls of the house. A number of deer are depicted; all are fallow, the majority of them appearing to be bucks, some of them against the building itself. Some cattle are also to be seen.[17]

Lord Sidmouth's major contribution to the park was trees, and it was he who introduced, in 1819, the systematic establishment of plantations, fenced to protect them from the deer. In some instances the fencing was removed at a later date and the plantation thrown open, Spanker's Hill Wood being an example. Planted in three sections in 1819, 1824 and 1877,[18] mainly with indigenous forest trees (although there are some sweet chestnuts), part of it was unfenced in 1909, and the remainder as recently as 1950. Some remain fenced and are today recognized as bird sanctuaries. The large Sidmouth Wood, named after the Viscount, is one. The area north of the driftway, which bisects the plantation from east to west, and through which the public can walk, was planted in 1823, and the

Right: White Lodge. The two states of Repton's 'hinged plate' illustrating his design for the garden on the west front. The 'hinge' is clearly visible on the second plate

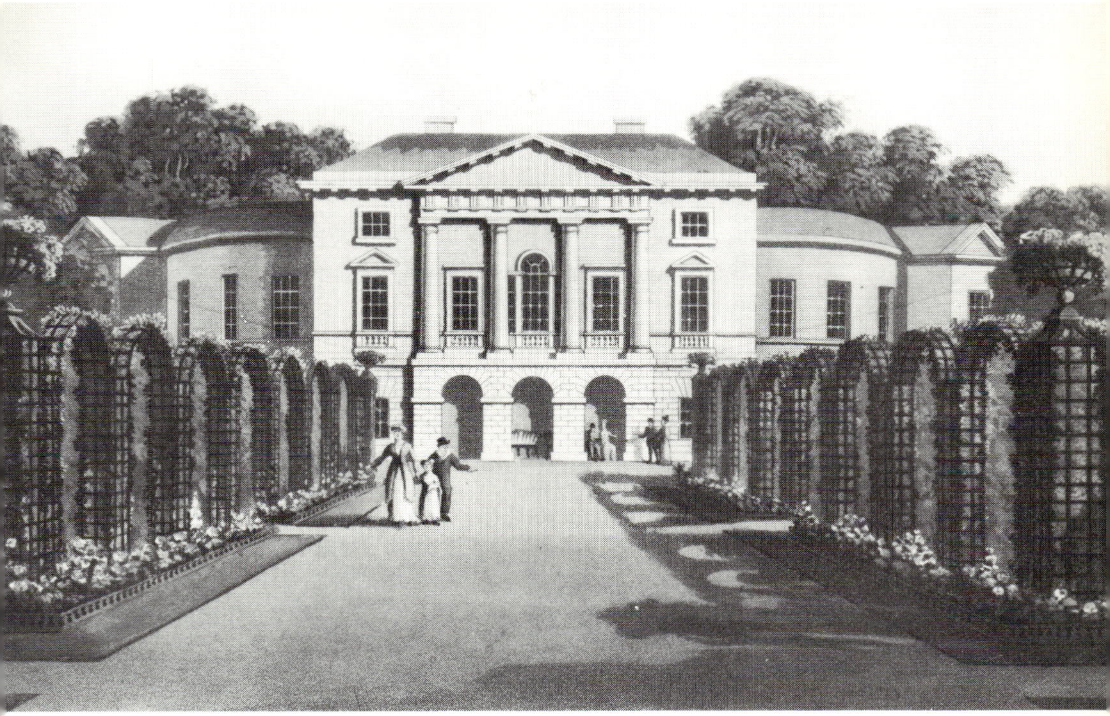

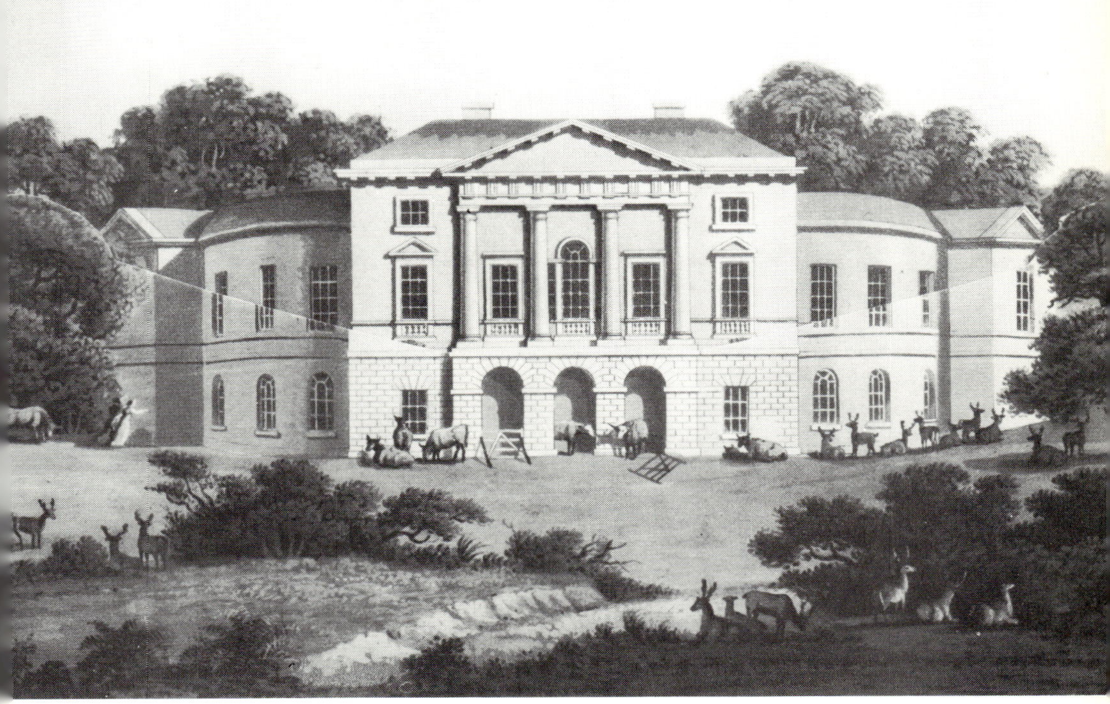

south end seven years later. The section in between has never been planted, and maps of the mid nineteenth century show the area as a 'game preserve', containing a few trees only, which were presumably extant when the plantation was first enclosed.[19] It is now heavily wooded with comparatively young trees, many of them birch which have established naturally.

Another plantation started by Lord Sidmouth was Isabella Plantation, a wood which was to become particularly well known in a later age. Viscount Sidmouth was to see only one section planted, in 1831; it was subsequently enlarged in 1845 and 1860, after his death.

It was during this period that Edward Jesse served as Surveyor of His Majesty's Parks and Palaces, and he, too, was to leave his mark on Richmond Park. Jesse was also a natural historian of note, and many of his observations are delightfully preserved in his *Gleanings of Natural History*, first published in 1834–5. Of the trees in the park he wrote that they 'were almost entirely oaks and some of them of very large dimensions. Many of them, however, are pollards, in consequence of a custom which formerly prevailed very generally of lopping trees for browse for the deer.'[20] He returns to the theme later: 'In former times it was the custom to cut down browse-wood for the deer in winter, and certain trees were marked for that purpose, and were generally lopped every seven years.'[21] Here is an explanation for the 'stag-headed' oaks which contribute so much to the character of the park.

Petersham Lodge and the adjacent grounds were leased to the Hydes in 1686 (Chapter 5) and were lost to the park. In 1721 the lodge was destroyed by fire, but it was rebuilt some years later by William Stanhope, Earl of Harrington, who then owned the lease. It was to change hands several times in the eighteenth century, one of the owners being the Duke of Clarence, later William IV (1830–37).[22] By the end of the century it was in the hands of Lord Huntingtower, a member of the Dysart family, who died in 1833. Jesse, in his official capacity, negotiated the return of the lodge and grounds to the park, and a price of £14,500 was agreed with the executors of Lord Huntingtower's estates.[23] In all some forty-one hectares of land were returned to the park; that is a large proportion of the area now known as Petersham Park.

An engraving of Petersham Lodge, dated 1720 and attributed to Kip, shows extensive formal gardens and orchards associated with the lodge, but no trace of them now remains. According to Jesse, the mature Lebanon cedars which still stand in Petersham Park and which were within the land belonging to the lodge, were probably planted as seedlings in about 1740 by John, second Duke of Argyle, who married a daughter of the Countess of Dysart by her first marriage, and occupied the neighbouring Sudbrook estate, a proportion of the grounds of which were originally

An old Pollard oak

New Parke in Surry the Seat of the R.: Hon.ble

Petersham Lodge before 1721 when the lodge was burnt down

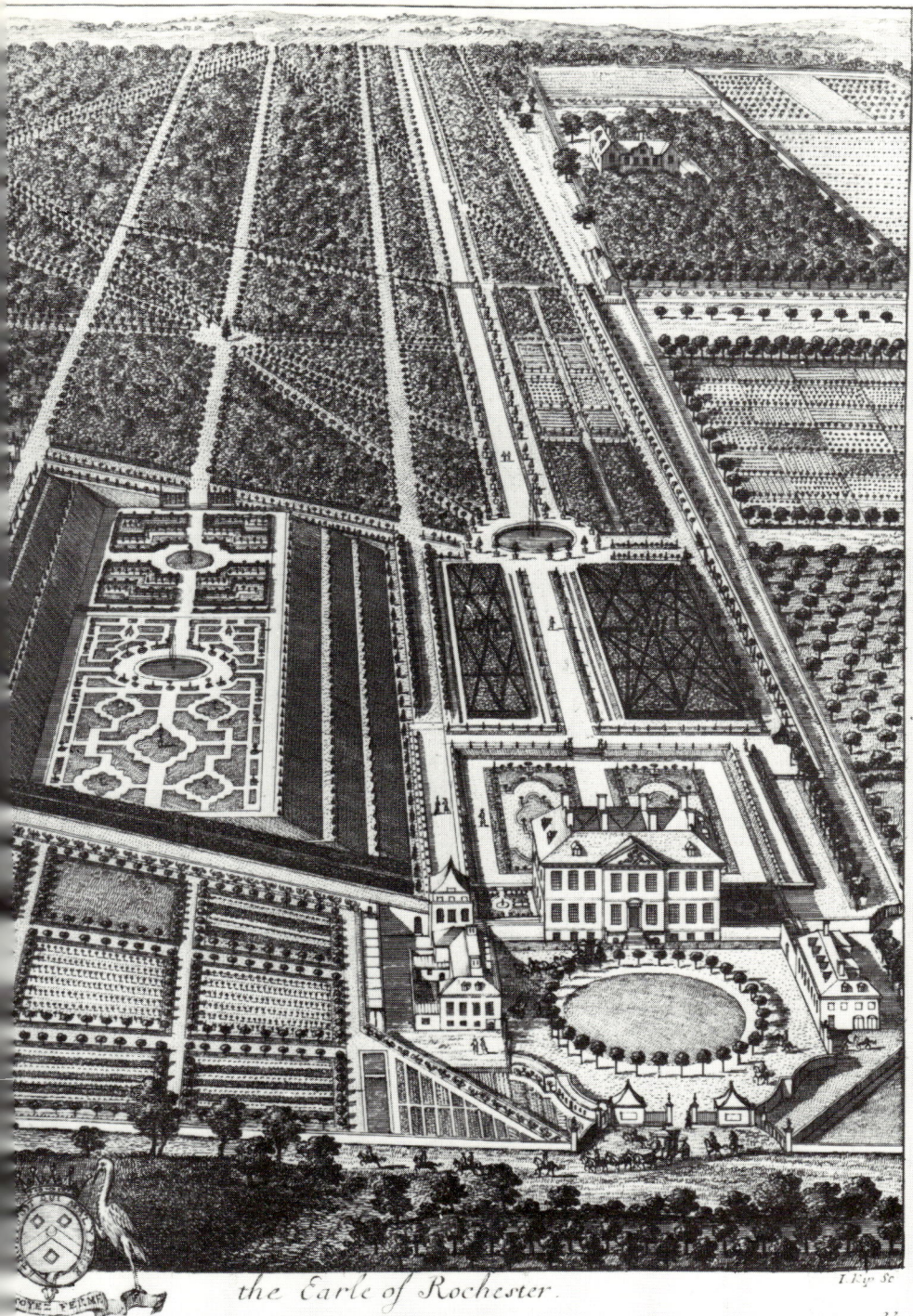

the Earle of Rochester.

I. Kip Sc

95

The restored lodge (this engraving was made in 1794)

part of Richmond Park.[24] One of the trees was so severely damaged during the harsh winter of 1981–2 that it subsequently had to be felled, and a 'ring count' of the stump suggested that the tree was then between 230 and 250 years old, which indicates that Jesse's supposition may well have been correct. Petersham Lodge was finally demolished in 1835, being by then in an advanced state of decay.

Concern about the problems of finding a sufficient supply of quality fallow venison to meet the demands of the Royal Venison Warrant prompted the Lords Commissioners of HM Treasury (who were responsible for the administration of the warrant) to commission a survey of the deer herds of the royal parks and forests in 1831. The officer selected to undertake the survey was none other than Edward Jesse, who set about the task in July of that year, royal approval for the survey having been granted by then. His report[25] was to be completed before the end of the year.

Jesse's first step was to send questionnaires to the rangers of the parks and forests in order to establish, amongst other matters, the strength of the various herds. By then many of the royal forests had been disafforested, and only the New Forest Hampshire, Wychwood Forest Oxfordshire, Whittlewood and Rockingham Forests Northamptonshire and Waltham Forest (a combination of the remaining sections of the ancient Epping and Hainault Forests of Essex) remained to come under his scrutiny. The parks involved were Richmond, Hampton Court, Bushy, Greenwich, Hyde Park and Great Windsor Park, all of which then carried deer herds. From the returns, Jesse was able to verify that there was a grand total of fifteen thousand fallow deer in the royal parks and forests.

The survey provides the first detailed record of the number of deer in Richmond Park since 1669. The fallow herd was 1,400 strong, 560 of which were described as 'antler' and 840 as 'rascal'. Of the fifty red deer, ten were described as 'antler'. In hunting parlance the term 'rascal' was used to describe a stag younger than five or six years, and not 'warrantable' for hunting, or alternatively a deer out of condition. In the context of the survey, however, it seems that the word was used to describe all deer without antlers – that is, the females, together with the fawns and calves. An average of a hundred bucks and seventy-five does were being culled for the royal warrant each year, and the annual casualty rate among the fallow deer was stated to be forty.

'The venison from this Park [Richmond] is of good quality. The Deer are well managed and there are several Paddocks for fattening them for His Majesty's use,' Jesse was confident enough to report. He went on to suggest that, 'The deer in Richmond Park might be increased without inconvenience from 1400 to 2000 . . . if there was an improvement to the

Park by drainage . . . the expenses of the improvement would be amply repaid in a few years by the increased annual value of the herbage.' Of Hyde Park, Jesse stated that, 'By Order of His late Majesty [George IV] the deer were reserved for the Royal Table' and that 'Some of them were killed with Dogs an evil which appears inseparably connected with the maintenance of Deer in a Park in the Metropolis.' The Hyde Park deer were all fallow, and then numbered 118. He was not impressed with the deer of the forests, which were described as being poor and badly managed, with the exception of Whittlewood, whose venison was reputed to be of excellent quality.

The first tangible results of the survey came fourteen months later, when a decision was taken to disperse the Hyde Park herd, which by then had been reduced to fifty-eight. On 8 February 1833 the deer were caught up, half being taken to Richmond Park and half to Hampton Court.

The keepers detailed to execute the Hyde Park transfer were James Sawyer of Richmond and his younger brother Rowe, then keeper of nearby Bushy Park. The first James Sawyer of Richmond Park had died in 1825 and was succeeded by his son, also named James. The succession was apparently not automatic, there having been a second candidate, John Lucas, who was then second keeper, the son of the head keeper who had died in 1795. According to one account, Lucas was offered the post but declined the invitation in favour of Sawyer, on the grounds that, had he accepted, he would have been obliged to occupy the head keeper's lodge, thereby turning the widow and family of the first James Sawyer out of their home, which they had by then lived in for thirty years. Princess Elizabeth, Ranger of the park, is reputed to have marked this generous act by presenting Lucas with an engraved silver cup in appreciation 'of his very generous and friendly conduct towards the family of his old friend and fellow-servant, the Late Mr Sawyer'.[26]

The two keepers were on friendly terms and regularly visited each other's lodges, the families sometimes dining together. They worked together for much of the time, sharing the work of killing and butchering deer for the royal warrant and delivering the carcasses personally to the recipients. Lucas was responsible for rearing pheasants to sustain the stock but both keepers joined in shooting pheasant and partridge for the royal table. One of Sawyer's duties was to meet and escort the King when he visited or passed through the park, and sometimes he was accompanied by Lucas on those occasions. On 20 August 1835 William IV lunched at Pembroke Lodge with the Earl of Erroll (then Master of the Royal Buckhounds and married to one of William IV's daughters by his mistress, Mrs Jordan), whose residence it was at that time, and afterwards Sawyer and Lucas rode with the King to Kew. Both were excellent horsemen and regularly attended meets of the Royal Buckhounds.

Perhaps they were obliged to do so, because their warrants as keepers still referred to their responsibility for the game ten miles around 'Our Royal Palaces, or usual places of residence, for our Royal Sport and Diversion'.[27]

Both Sawyer and Lucas kept personal assistants, whom they paid from their own pockets, to aid them with their duties. Lucas's son, another John, was one; indeed his second son was also in training as a keeper and may too have served in the park as an assistant. Additionally, there were two gamekeepers, one who lived at Ladderstile Lodge, and the second at Bishop's Lodge, a few hundred yards north of Richmond Gate. Bishop's Lodge, which dates from the early nineteenth century, was built as a gamekeeper's residence. A William Bishop was personal assistant to Sawyer's father by 1789,[28] and Charles Bishop is mentioned as a gamekeeper in 1806 and again in 1827.[29] The two Bishops were probably related and, in line with tradition, gave their name to the lodge.[28] In 1835 there is a record of three gamekeepers, by name Baker, Plank and Turner, but one of those may have been an assistant. Of the remainder of the permanent staff of the time, there were five gatekeepers (one of whom, Blandford, was also park carpenter), the park bailiff, responsible for the agricultural and general maintenance work, two carters and a number of labourers, three of whom were members of a family named Neal.

8

The Park – into the Victorian Years

Rowe Sawyer, he who assisted his elder brother, James Sawyer, to move the Hyde Park deer in 1833, was assistant to Mr Elphick, deer-keeper at Bushy Park, who died in January 1831. On learning of this event, James Sawyer took the coach to Brighton, where he was granted an audience with the King, William IV, at the Pavilion, the result of which was the promotion of Rowe to the deer-keeper's position at Bushy.[1] The King, in fact, knew the Sawyer family well, having come into contact with them, when, as Duke of Clarence, he was resident in Petersham Lodge.[2] The Sawyer family were represented in other deer parks too: another brother, Henry Charles, was deerkeeper to the Duke of Bedford at Woburn Bedfordshire, and his aunt Mary was married to William Tetshall, deer-keeper to the Earl of Essex at Cassiobury Park Hertfordshire.[3]

The family association was to be useful in a series of introductions and exchanges of deer involving Richmond and other royal parks between 1833 and 1853. This vast movement of deer – large numbers were involved, all fallow – was in direct response to Jesse's survey of 1831, the object being to build up the herds of the parks to a degree which would enable the requirements of the Royal Venison Warrant to be comfortably met. The Hyde Park deer were not the only ones to be moved in 1833. Deer were exchanged with Woburn and Cassiobury Parks. James Sawyer noted in his diary that Friday 1 March 1833 was 'a very fine morning', part of which he spent catching 'three brace of deer sorels and sores for Woburn Park'. Tuesday 16 April that year started with 'a dull morning' and saw John Lucas, the second or under keeper returning from Cassiobury with 'eight brace [of deer] in exchange'. On Saturday 20 April it was again 'a fine morning', and Sawyer 'caught three brace of deer for the exchange. They ran amazingly and we had some rare galloping.'[1]

Catching live deer for transporting elsewhere (or, in the case of bucks required for venison, for confining in stalls) was not a simple task. One method used involved two or three keepers, on horseback and each with a dog, riding down and cutting out from the herd a selected animal. As soon as it had been cut out, the dogs were sent in pursuit, supported by younger dogs, which were 'slipped' as soon as the keepers' dogs had been laid on. Once the animal had been brought to bay, the dogs seized it by throat and ears, holding it until the keepers arrived. The deer was then immobilized by strapping hind and forelegs together, and loaded onto the horse-drawn van following behind. The dogs were trained to pull deer down and detain them without causing injury, and they are described as 'a large rough sort of greyhound, and very powerful and sagacious'.[4] Powerful they must have been, for they were also used to capture stags for the Royal Hunt paddocks. An alternative method used the reward of food to entice deer into paddocks. 'Toils' were erected at selected openings in the paddock rails, the nets being supported on stout poles about two metres high. Dogs were then introduced into the paddocks, their job being to drive chosen animals into the nets, in which they became entangled, thus enabling them to be quickly immobilized.

For many of the moves, however, a professional was employed, doubtless because of the large number of animals involved. W. Herring was in business as an 'Importer of red and fallow deer to Her Majesty and dealer in all sorts of Pheasant, Fancy poultry, Swan and Waterfowl, Gold and Silver Fish, Sporting and Fancy Dogs' and operated from 'The Menagerie, New Road, near Regent's Park'.[5]

His first commission for the Commissioners of Woods etc. was a small one: the supply of seven bucks from an undisclosed source for Richmond Park in 1833. His next, two years later, was on a larger scale. The Earl Spencer gifted his entire herd of fallow deer in Althorp Park, Northamptonshire, to William IV, and it was Herring's task to catch up and transport them to various royal parks. A large proportion, 269 in all, were safely received at Richmond.[5] Herring lost only fifteen deer (he made no charge for those that died) in the whole operation, a fact which suggests that he was not without expertise and ability in his profession. Althorp Park was restocked with deer about 1846, the deer being fallow of a chocolate-brown colour from Dingley Park, near Market Harborough.[6]

Another large herd of fallow came to the park in 1843. Lord Sidmouth offered the fallow deer of Stowell Park, Gloucestershire – the country seat of his second wife – to Queen Victoria, 'provided that it should be added to the Royal Herd in Richmond Park, which offer Her Majesty was pleased to accept'. Herring successfully moved the herd in March of that year, charging 10 shillings a head for the 179 animals. From Hartlebury Park, Worcestershire came twenty bucks in the same year, presented to the Queen by the Bishop of Worcester. Three years later the Queen received yet another gift of fallow deer for the royal parks, this time from the Earl of Ducie's Woodchester Park. Of the two-hundred-strong herd, sixty came to Richmond. A small number went to Phoenix Park, Dublin – then a royal park – and a contingent was destined for the New Forest, to which destination they could not be directly sent: the Forest Keepers had first to 'kill off some of their poorer deer to make room for those from the Earl of Ducie', so they were temporarily paddocked in Richmond Park.[5] The keepers may not have been pleased to see them when they did arrive at the forest, because the thirteen brace from Woodchester sent to Windsor Great Park were reported to have been received there in very poor condition.[7] On the other hand, their brief sojourn at Richmond may have been sufficient to restore the New Forest contingent to good condition before they set out on the final leg of their journey!

In 1847 ten brace of does were purchased from the Duke of Norfolk's Arundel Park (Sussex), and the following year another batch of ten brace were sent – in this instance as a gift. The exchange of small numbers of deer between the various royal parks herds was not uncommon, but the transfer of fifty fallow from Great Windsor Park to Richmond in 1848 was unusual. This great movement of fallow deer came to an end in 1853, when Whittlewood and Wychwood Forests were disafforested (Stats 14 & 15 Vic. C76), and the deer of the forests – those which could be caught up – distributed among the royal parks. From this source Richmond received 150 males and fifty females.

It seems that not all of those transfers were carried out with proper authority. In 1850 Herring delivered twenty bucks to Richmond from the Earl of Verulam's Gorhambury Park, Hertfordshire. A few months later Sawyer received a letter from the Office of Woods, requiring him to explain who had authorized this acquisition.[7] An explanation may have been offered, but no record of it remains. Perhaps there had been a bureaucratic blunder!

Despite this large influx of fallow deer, there was little increase in the size of the park herds. Jesse's survey of 1831 revealed the presence of 1,400 animals; in 1848 a census put the numbers at '1,500 or there abouts'.[5] This census was carried out in January, in which month a more accurate count could be made, because much of the ground-level vegetation, such as bracken, would by then have died back. The 1831 count, on the other hand, was taken during the summer, when ground-cover vegetation would be lush and thick, offering ample concealment for the deer, particularly fawns. The difference in numbers, therefore, may have been much closer than available records indicate.

The 1848 census, made by Sawyer, was detailed, identifying the deer by age and sex. Excluding fawns, there were 700 males and 550 females, a rather odd ratio when compared with modern thought, which suggests that the most desirable ratio in deer and other ungulates is two mature males to five mature females. However, the Commissioners of HM Woods etc. had laid down a policy in 1843 which required the keepers to achieve a ratio of five males to three females, having been advised that, 'In some of the best managed herds in the country the number of male deer was nearly double that of the female.' This policy was pursued with some vigour, even to the extent of killing off 'such proportion of female fawns dropped . . . as shall tend to produce the object in view'. The policy was to be followed for many years – in fact until the 1920s, although the practice of killing newly born fawns for this purpose was stopped well before the turn of the century – but the desired ratio was never quite achieved.

It was during this period that the management of the fallow herds reached its peak of intensity – it had, in effect, become a deer-farming operation, one manifestation of which was the appearance of an increased number of deer enclosures, or pens, in the park. In 1754 there were but two, one immediately to the south-west of White Ash Lodge, the second against the boundary wall, midway between Ham and Kingston Gates.[8] Less than a hundred years later there were five. Predictably one was adjacent to the head keeper's lodge, another near White Ash Lodge (but to the north-east). A third was close to White Lodge, and the other two were in the south of the park. The two pens of the previous century had gone.[9] The primary purpose of the pens was to enable the herds to be fed with supplementary foodstuffs during winter, when the grazing was poor, but they were also used for confining selected deer at other times of the year, for a variety of reasons.

Each pen was a little over 2½ acres (one hectare) in area, surrounded by post and rail fencing, so designed that deer could enter and leave at will, but not the cattle at large in the park. Within the pen was a smaller enclosure, the entrance to which was protected by a 'fawn gate', a device which allowed fawns, but not adult deer, access to the inner enclosure. This enabled the fawns to be fed apart from the adults, thus ensuring that they received their due proportion of food. The inner sanctum also housed a brick-built shed, used for food storage.[10] Today all that remains of the pens are two simple, fenced enclosures, one near White Lodge, the other in High Wood. The pens are no longer used for their original purpose, but they are worthy of retention as a tangible reminder of the past.

There were about four deer for every five acres (two hectares) of open parkland. Although the pastures were sufficient to sustain that stocking rate, plus a limited number of cattle (for which the grazing rent was 2s. 6d. a week per beast) from spring to autumn, supplementary winter feeding was a regular feature of herd management. Hay, beans, corn, carrots, potatoes and acorns were all part of the winter diet. Only the hay was produced – in the large paddocks on the east side of the Beverley Brook –

and the acorns gathered in the park (from time to time attempts were made to grow other crops for deer feed, apparently with little success). In some years over a hundred loads of hay, each load weighing a little over a tonne, were mown and ricked, at an estimated cost of about a third of the market price. Other produce was bought locally. Beans, of which more than thirty tonnes were consumed annually, cost in the region of £8 a tonne. In 1840 the cost of supplementary feeding for the deer was £717. 19s. 9d.,[11] and some idea of the cost of maintaining a stall-fed buck can be gleaned from the cost of foraging a horse in the royal mews, which in that year was £2 a month.[12] For gathering acorns (and horse chestnuts) in the park for deer feed, small boys were employed – including the head keeper's sons![13]

When the time came to turn stall-fed bucks into venison, they were simply shot through the head, with a rifle, from an open window in the shed in which they were kept. Paddocked bucks were also head-shot with a rifle, usually from a range of ten to thirty metres. Sometimes the keeper would climb a convenient tree in the paddock, towards which the bucks could be gently driven, so that he could safely and efficiently dispatch them. The does were a different proposition. They were usually killed in the open parkland, shot through the heart.[14]

Selecting and killing does, even within the confines of a park, is not easy. By the time the doe season opened in November, the does, together with fawns and immature animals, had gathered into large herds. Nervous and skittish, a herd would move off, and perhaps even bolt, at anything untoward, usually led by an old, experienced doe. One shot could be sufficient to ensure that a herd would be careful to remain out of gunshot range for the rest of the day. So an ancient method was employed of directing the animals into a pre-selected location, from which they could be ambushed by waiting keepers. A herd was gently moved into the vicinity of the chosen location by one or two horsemen. There, long lengths of twine, on which feathers or coloured rags were knotted at intervals (variously known as suelling, sewelling or shewel; James Sawyer used the term 'tats' to describe them), had been laid out beforehand. As the deer approached, small boys who were employed specially for the purpose, raised and shook the lengths of twine, thereby channelling the animals past the waiting guns.

Left: Two nineteenth-century scenes of feeding the deer during severe weather

Overleaf: Feeding the deer in the winter of 1968

The carcasses were butchered in the park, there being venison houses for hanging them at the head keeper's lodge, and that of the second keeper. The animals were shot about ten days before being dressed for the table and were usually delivered to Royal Venison Warrant recipients by either Sawyer or Lucas. Sometimes particularly fine animals were killed; one, shot on 25 June 1835 by Sawyer, was described as 'a very fat buck in weight 17 stone 3 lb. The skin weighed 13 lb. the haunches when cut up weighed 33 lb. each or 66 lb., the two divided down the back.' Unwanted fawns were killed off in August, and on 28 August – 'a very fine morning' – Sawyer himself shot five, and one of the gamekeepers, Turner by name, four.[15]

Sometimes matters did not go according to plan, as happened on Wednesday 2 September 1829, which was another 'fine day', when Sawyer shot at a buck on 'the lawn' below Barn Wood (the *laund* of the medieval park or forest. The ancient meaning of this word is perpetuated in 'the Lawn Plantation', the wood between Spanker's Hill car-park and the Pen Ponds, planted in 1883). He knocked it over without killing the animal; it was not even seriously injured and was quickly back on its feet and away. The head keeper returned to his lodge to collect two of his dogs, Spring and Ratler, who soon picked up the trail. They cornered the buck near the Venison House yard (adjacent to Sawyer's Lodge), but the animal successfully defended itself and escaped, after injuring Spring by pinning him against a wooden post. Another keeper's dog was called in as a replacement, and the buck was again brought to bay a few hundred yards away, and killed.[16]

The deer and game-keepers were required to be first-class shots, and when they were not shooting deer – for which purpose both smooth-bore and rifled guns were used – game or vermin, they practised regularly. One of the head keeper's many duties was to accompany guests invited to shoot or fish in the park. In May 1836, when he was shooting with Lord Vernon, this distinguished guest shot a thrush (apparently thrushes and starlings were occasionally used for target practice) and a rabbit, 'but missed some good shots in the course of the day'. Sawyer, however, 'made capital shot at a spot on a thorn tree at 100 yards' and had no doubt that 'my gun shoots faster than Lord Vernon's his bore being larger and his shooting less powder'.[17]

What gun this was is not recorded. Perhaps it was a family heirloom, passed down from Sawyer's great-uncle, Henry Sawyer of Petworth Park, who designed and patented a breach-loading gun in 1787.[18] Breach-loading guns were not new – primitive breach-loading canons were in use in the fifteenth century, and Henry VIII had at least two breach-loading long guns – but it was not until the second half of the eighteenth century that the popularity of breach-loading rifles grew in British military circles,[19] and it seems possible that Henry Sawyer could have adapted a sporting gun from a military model.

Recently a considerable quantity of lead projectiles were discovered in a small group of old oaks close to White Ash Lodge. Their size and shape suggest that they were rifle or musket balls, which may have been fired into the trees by way of target practice. A number of them were forwarded to the Armouries at the Tower of London for examination. Although the projectiles are deformed, expert opinion was that their original shape was almost certainly spherical, which indicated that they date from the first half of the nineteenth century or earlier. They are between sixteen and twenty bore and were probably fired from a flintlock or percussion sporting rifle.[20] In the early years of the nineteenth century the most popular rifle for deer was the sixteen bore (.662 calibre), which fired a ball weighing one ounce.[21] The keepers bought their own powder and shot – they may well have made their own projectiles by pouring lead into prepared moulds – and in the year 1870–71 the head keeper's official allowance for those purchases was £12.[22]

9

The Park – to the Late Nineteenth Century

A few years after the accession of George III, a responsibility outside the confines of the park was placed on the park bailiff, that of the superintendence of the Richmond to Kew road. This came about by an Act of Parliament (6 Geo. III C71) designed to provide work for the unemployed of Richmond. The park bailiff supervised the work, which included, as well as the repair of the road and pavements, and the maintenance of roadside trees, cleaning, lighting and policing the road.[1]

During the latter years of the eighteenth century, after the Court of George III had been established at Kew, and the first half of the nineteenth, the 'Kew Cart' made regular journeys along this road, travelling between Richmond, Kew and Windsor Castle. On the cart was carried produce from Richmond Park, destined for the royal table. Pheasant, partridge, hares and leverets, and sometimes fish, were sent, as in May 1836, when three brace of carp were requested.[2] A substantial quantity of game was then shot in the park: 188 brace of pheasant, 56½ brace of partridge and 180 hares in 1838.[3] Not all went to the royal table; there were shooting parties organized by the Ranger and others, hares were also coursed, and no doubt the participants all had some share in the 'bag'.

The head keeper was required to arrange shooting, coursing and fishing for invited guests from time to time. On 20 October 1836 a Mr Laurence 'came and coursed 2½ brace (of hares) were killed'. Just over a week later Sawyer was again coursing, this time with a Mr Basildon, and '2 brace were killed and had some of the best runs I have seen for some time'. In August the same year Sir F. Chantry, when fishing with a friend in the park, caught a 6 lb fish. What kind of fish it was is not recorded. It may well have been a carp, a species which was apparently plentiful, for there were sufficient of them to enable Sawyer to send 68 brace to stock the waters of Bushy Park in June of that year.[4] That the park ponds were maintained for

White Lodge, the East Front

fish production, just as they were in a medieval deer park, is clear from a royal command communicated to Sawyer in November 1825. The King (William IV) instructed him to ensure that the stock of fish in the park was properly kept up. He was to obtain fish for stocking from unidentified sources, 'the sort and quantity of fish His Majesty leaves to your [Sawyer's] discretion'.[5]

During the latter years of his tenure as Deputy Ranger, Lord Sidmouth seems to have been content to let his head keeper take over much of the burden of managing the park. Sawyer was expected to report to Lord Sidmouth regularly, however, and he visited the Deputy Ranger's residence several times a month, usually at 10 a.m. Sometimes he attended to personal matters for his lordship. For instance, in June 1836 he arranged for the provision of 'branches of oak and thorn and horse chestnut' for decorating a local infant school on the occasion of their annual fête – a school in which one of Sidmouth's daughters, Charlotte, had a particular interest. Two years earlier he had carried out a less pleasant task, that of destroying the Deputy Ranger's dogs after they had been attacked in the park by what was reputedly a mad (rabid) dog. That Sawyer held Lord Sidmouth in high esteem is evident from a message he had prepared on 30 June 1831, to be delivered, in the event of his early death, to one of his brothers. 'In Lord Sidmouth', he wrote, 'you will find a very good and earnest friend to the family – a man to who you may open your heart for Fatherly friendship.'[6] In fact, Sawyer comfortably outlived Lord Sidmouth, who died at White Lodge in 1844.

The Deputy Ranger's office remained vacant for eleven years after the death of Lord Sidmouth, and Sawyer reported directly to the Ranger. In 1835 the first Duke of Cambridge had been appointed to that office, succeeding his sister Princess Elizabeth. His warrant of appointment gave him the custody of the deer, game, fish, gates and other royalties. He was also responsible for the recruitment, and dismissal when necessary, of the deer and gamekeepers, park- and gate-keepers. But he had no control over lodges, with the exception of nominating staff for lodge tenancies, buildings, drives and walks (paths and tracks), nor authority over the soil, herbage (except for the pastures) or timber. Responsibility for those remained firmly in the hands of the Office of Woods. The Ranger was required to produce accounts of revenue and expenditure to the Commissioners of Woods every quarter. For this he received 6 shillings a day, paid quarterly, the occupation of White Lodge, three bucks and three does each season, and the right to 'depasture as many cows as shall be exclusively in his own keeping'.[7] In fact, the Duke of Cambridge did not take up residence in White Lodge, for it was still the home of Lord Sidmouth. Old Lodge, then in poor condition, was considered as an alternative, but the cost of repairing the building 'as a Residence suited to the Occupation of HRH The Ranger' was too great, and the Duke was given Cambridge Cottage, Kew, as his official residence. He also owned property outside the park, having acquired the Coombe Estate (previously Coombe Nevill Manor) from the third Earl Spencer in 1837.[7a] There were then three farms on the estate, from which some of the winter feed for the park deer herds was purchased.

Princess Mary, Duchess of Gloucester and fourth daughter of George III, took up residence at White Lodge when it fell vacant in 1844. On the death of the Duke of Cambridge six years later, the Princess was appointed Ranger in his place. White Lodge became, once again, the official home of the park Ranger.

Sheen Cottage. This house was probably developed from the 'Dog Kennel' of the Walpole era

From Pembroke Lodge to Petersham Park

In 1851 the amalgamation of the Office of Works and Public Buildings and the Office of Woods (Chapter 7) was reversed, and public buildings, together with the royal palaces and parks, were placed under a separate First Commissioner of Works (Stats 14 & 15 Vic. C42). This still left a somewhat cumbersome administrative structure, because the Ranger, officially at least, retained considerable authority over the affairs of the park, and the Lords Commissioners of HM Treasury remained involved, via their responsibility for administering the Royal Venison Warrant.

Not all the lodges were occupied by staff. The 'Dog Kennel' of Walpole's time was developed into a residence of some standing. In the late eighteenth and first half of the nineteenth centuries it was occupied by the Adam family (the Rt Hon. William Adam was High Commissioner for Scotland in the reign of George IV, and his son the Accountant General of the Court of Chancery), who gave their name to the still existing pond immediately to the south of the lodge. In 1852 Sir Richard Owen, the first Director of the Natural History Museum (Kensington) and a scientist of note, was granted the property by Queen Victoria.[8] In 1847 the Queen granted Pembroke Lodge to her Prime Minister, Lord John Russell, and although he was to die in 1878, the family remained in occupation until 1929.[9] Bertrand Russell, the philosopher and Lord John's grandson, spent much of his childhood there. Lord John took considerable interest in his surroundings, and in April 1856 he wrote to the head keeper, requesting him to stop 'boys playing cricket in all sorts of weathers in Petersham Park thus damaging the turf and greatly disturbing the deer who are attracted to this area it having the best herbage in the Park'.[10] A further lodge was added to the park's stock of buildings in the early 1850s. This was Oak Lodge, built at the south end of Sidmouth Plantation for the park bailiff.

Public access to the park remained restricted for much of the nineteenth century. During the first fifty years or so, pedestrians appear to have been largely confined to the roads and footpaths, carriages could enter only if they carried a 'card of admission', issued by Sawyer on behalf of the Ranger, and dogs could not be brought in. Poaching was a continuing problem, the poachers' targets probably being game and rabbits rather than deer. The park labourers could add to their earnings by night watching against poachers, and during the breeding season horsemen were employed for 'bird minding' in the larger plantations.[11] In the spring of 1854 a guest who had been lunching with Lord and Lady Russell at Pembroke Lodge was held up by a youth armed with a pistol as she was leaving the park and relieved of her watch and jewellery. This incident reputedly led to the establishment of a park police force,[12] but other considerations, such as the bailiff's responsibility for policing the road beween Richmond and Kew, were also doubtless involved.

The red deer herd was kept relatively static during those years, averaging around fifty animals. Its *raison d'être* was the provision of deer, mostly stags, for the Royal Hunt paddocks at Swinley.[13] One curious circumstance arose in 1825, when not a single calf was born, although the hinds had bred freely the preceding year and did so in subsequent years.[14] Halfway through the century, however, at least two Richmond Park red deer were destined to travel well beyond Swinley.

Red deer were first introduced into New Zealand in 1850, when Lord Petre sent a stag and a hind to his brother, the Hon. H. W. Petre, who was then resident in Nelson, South Island. The deer came from Lord Petre's Thorndon Hall Park in Essex. The hind was killed shortly after being liberated into its new territory and, on learning of this, the Prince Consort

A Richmond Park stag and two hinds

arranged for a stag and hind to be sent from Richmond Park as replacements. The stag was safely delivered, but the hind did not survive the voyage. In 1860, Lord Petre sent out a further stag and two hinds from Thorndon Hall, all of which safely reached their destination. Those animals were the progenitors of the red deer herds of the Nelson and Marlborough districts in the north of South Island.[15]

Further south, the Rakaia red deer herd, known for the superior body weight of the stags, and the quality of their antlers, originated from deer sent out from Stoke Park, Buckinghamshire in 1897.[16] The basis of the Stoke Park herd was reputedly the red deer of Windsor Forest, and of Stoke Park Whitaker noted that, 'Some of the finest red stags weigh nearly 20 stone, being unusually large.'[17] The Rakaia herd today has been influenced by infiltration from the Nelson and Marlborough herds from the north, and from the south by descendants of Scottish Highland deer released in the Otago area in 1871. (The Otago Acclimatization Society obtained twenty red deer from the Earl of Dalhousie in 1870, the first consignment of eight calves coming from Mark Forest.)[18] Windsor deer

are also represented in the North Island. In 1862 the Prince Consort presented a stag and two hinds from the Great Park to the people of New Zealand. The animals were successfully released near Taratahi, Carleton, and were the nucleus of the Wiararapa herd of North Island.[15]

Fallow deer from Richmond Park were among those shipped from Gravesend on board the *Thorland Castle* in November 1876. The consignment was made up of thirty-two animals, of which ten were from Richmond, and the remainder from Carshalton Park (Surrey). All but four survived the voyage. There is also record of three fallow, a buck and two does, having been sent from Richmond Park in 1864.

Pressure continued to be exerted on the park's fallow herds by the demands made on them for the provision of venison for the royal warrant. Other traditional sources of supply were drying up, one by one. The New Forest fell by the wayside with the Disafforestation Act of 1851 (Stats 14 & 15 Vic. C76), and Whittlewood and Wychwood Forests followed suit two years later (Stats 16 & 17 Vic. C36 & 42). The Epping Forest Act of 1872 saw the last of the royal forests go, leaving the royal parks as the only remaining sources of supply.

In an attempt to increase venison production, a decision was taken to improve the drainage of Richmond Park, one of the major recommendations made by Jesse in his survey of 1831. In 1856 a land-drainage expert, Mr Josiah Parks, was commissioned to design and introduce an extensive system of land drains covering some 1,300 acres (500 hectares). The work, which included the creation of nine new ponds as watering places for the deer, was completed by 1861, at a cost of £8,776.[19] It seems unlikely that the drains made any significant difference to the low-lying, marshy areas of the park, but they probably improved the quality of the better pasture lands. Over the years many of the drains have been blocked and disrupted by tree roots, or have otherwise deteriorated, but fragmented parts of the system have withstood the test of time and, to some degree, remain effective.

The intensive management of the fallow herds practised in the nineteenth century included regular pasture husbandry, and in the year 1870–71 the cost of 'dressing grassland in the open part of the Park' was £250, a sixth of the total maintenance expenditure incurred by the park bailiff's department for that year.[20] 'Spudding thistles, etc.' and 'spreading cow manure' on the pastures were routine chores. Bracken was cut from selected areas annually, for stacking and drying prior to being used for winter bedding for the horses and cattle.[21] Bracken was also probably cut from the margins of the pastures, to prevent its encroachment into the grasslands.

The Lords Commissioners were concerned not only about the problems of finding a sufficient supply of venison for the royal warrant but also about the cost of producing it. In 1871 'The Keeper of each Park was requested (by the Lords Commissioners) to state what he fairly considered to be the value of the grazings of the Park provided that no deer were kept therein; from this sum was deducted the annual amount at present realised by grazing rents and to the difference was added the amount of additional expenditure incurred annually in procuring hay and corn as food for the deer; this sum being divided by the number of deer annually distributed affording an approximate cost to the Consolidated Fund of each deer given away.' Not surprisingly, the estimated costs varied wildly. Greenwich Park, for example, provided an average of five deer a year from its small herd at a cost of £19. 4s. 0d. a head, whereas Richmond was providing 165 a year at a cost of only £9. 14s. 0d.[22]

However, the Lords Commissioners were apparently satisfied that the estimates which they received from the various parks were sufficiently accurate for their purpose. After due consideration, they concluded that, 'The chief cost to the public is entailed by the maintenance of the deer in these Parks (the Royal Parks) and that the actual value of the grants of venison is comparatively slight. Their Lordships considering the great addition which the presence of the herds make to the beauty of the Parks are not prepared to direct that they should be removed.' Nor did their lordships consider it advisable to disturb the arrangements involving the distribution of venison by royal warrant.[23] Here is a significant watershed in the history of Richmond Park, because, had their lordships come to the opposite conclusion – had they decided to recommend that the deer should be removed – the park might well have been a very different place today. Without the presence of the deer herds, could the park have survived intact?

In 1872 the first Royal Parks and Gardens Regulations Act (Stats 31 & 32, Vic. C15) was passed by Parliament: clear indication that public access to the royal parks, including Richmond, was becoming much less restrained. The preamble to the Act sums up the purpose of the regulations: 'Whereas it is expedient to protect from injury the Royal parks, gardens and possessions under the management of the Commissioners of Her Majesty's Works and Public Buildings, herein after called the Commissioners, and to secure the public from molestation and annoyance while enjoying such parks, gardens and possessions . . .'. There was already a small force of park police attached to Richmond Park, and the Act increased their authority by requiring them to be attested as constables before a Justice of the Peace.

Financial accounts for the year 1870–71 record that the head park constable was paid £1. 5s. 0d. a week, and the three park constables under him one guinea. They were provided with uniforms costing eight guineas each, but it is not recorded how long the uniforms were expected to last!

Cattle in Martin's Pond, one of the nine new ponds dug between 1856–61. On the horizon is the windmill on Wimbledon Common

View from Ham Gate by J. de Koster (1767–1831)

Red deer at play – Ham Dip Pond. This was one of the ponds dug between 1856–61

Additionally, three *police* constables came under the park bailiff's jurisdiction, while the five gatekeepers were in the department of the Ranger. Four were paid £40 per year, whilst the Richmond gatekeeper received £60; perhaps he was also the carpenter, as one of the gatekeepers had been earlier in the century (see Chapter 7, page 99). However, they enjoyed rent-free accommodation (the park constables lived outside the park), being obliged to occupy the lodges at their respective gates. They wore the same uniform as the constables but were probably not attested as such under the 1872 Act. The same accounts[24] provide further evidence of easier public access – £125 was spent on 'sweeping, cleaning public conveniences, etc.'.

Although the Parks and Gardens Regulations Act suggests that the park was now managed as one unit by the Commissioners of Works, it seems that, in practice, the situation was rather more complicated. On the death of Princess Mary in 1857, George, second Duke of Cambridge, was appointed Ranger (Pat. Roll 21 Vic. Part 1, No. 16). His warrant of appointment was much the same as that of Princess Mary, except that he was not given the sole right to appoint deer-, game- and park-keepers; such appointments had also to be authorized by the Queen or by the Lords Commissioners of HM Treasury (but not by the Commissioners of Works).[25] Thus the management structure was to remain much as it had been, the Ranger's department and that of the park bailiff (which was directly responsible to the Office of Works) having separate areas of responsibility until the turn of the century. As with previous Rangers, day-to-day affairs were left in the hands of the Deputy Ranger, an office occupied between 1870 and 1898[26] by Major-General T. H. Clifton (who succeeded Colonel A. Liddell, Deputy Ranger between 1855 and 1870).

The year 1872 saw another event of note: the retirement of the head keeper, James Sawyer, after forty-two years in office. He was succeeded by his son, Henry George, then thirty-one years old, who was a junior gamekeeper in the park. John Lucas, who had in 1825 refused the head keeper's position in favour of James Sawyer, had died in the interim period, and his position as second keeper was filled by his son, also named John. His retirement in 1877 marked the end of the Lucas family's association with the park – an association which had continued, unbroken, since the reign of George I.[27]

One of the many changes which James Sawyer had witnessed in his long career was the erosion of the perquisites, some of them of considerable antiquity, which he and his predecessors had enjoyed. Their loss had been compensated for by increases in salary, and in the year of Sawyer's retirement his was £250 a year, plus allowances of £96 'in lieu of fees' (see Chapter 3) and £12 for the purchase of powder and shot. The keepers still enjoyed rent-free accommodation, and the right to maintain a limited number of cattle etc. for their personal use. One perquisite which was to survive for a few more years was that of selling rabbits. Reputedly, this was so valuable to the keepers that the rabbits were assiduously protected, much to the annoyance of local equestrians, for whom rabbit warrens and burrows were a menace.[28]

The grave of one John Sherratt is in Petersham churchyard, and the inscription on his tombstone carries the information that he was '28 years superintendent of Richmond Park' (probably from the 1850s to the late 1870s; precise dates of his service do not seem to have been recorded). The description is misleading, because the title of superintendent, in relation to the park, was not introduced until 1904, and the office which he undoubtedly held was that of park bailiff, who, as one of his several responsibilities, had the *superintendence* of the Richmond to Kew road. This was a responsibility which the park was to endure for only a few more years; in two agreements, dated 1880 and 1882, the Office of Works handed over to the Vestices of Richmond and Kew responsibility for the continuing maintenance of this road.[1]

The park bailiff also had the duty of supervising the maintenance of the park's trees, and the policy of the systematic establishment of plantations, introduced early in the century by Lord Sidmouth, was enthusiastically continued. The southern sections of Isabella Plantation were planted in 1861 and 1865; the west and south sections of Pen Pond Plantation in 1865; the Sawpit Plantations, one on either side of the west end of Queen's Ride (thus extending the length of the Ride), were planted in 1874–5, and the north-east section of Spanker's Hill Wood in 1877.[29] (The Sawpit Plantations were so called because of the presence of 'sawpits' in the locality. Sawpits were long, deep pits over which bulk timber was longitudinally placed for sawing with a two-man cross-cut saw, one man working below, in the pit, the second above ground. Then, as now, the park made full use of its own resources.)

The beech trees flanking the terrace walk between Richmond Gate and Pembroke Lodge gardens were probably planted shortly after Petersham Park was returned to its 'parent' in 1834. Hornbeam Walk, which runs from the south of Pembroke Lodge to Ham Cross Roads, may have been planted at about the same time as a continuation of the terrace walk, but the first record of its presence is not made until 1875.[30] A nursery for raising oaks was established in the park in 1824, but production was insufficient to cater for the large planting programmes, and young trees were acquired from other sources. Three thousand Spanish chestnut from A. Robertson of Dorking, and five hundred English oak from Veitch & Sons, were purchased in 1875. In the same year, two thousand oaks and five thousand 'firs' (possibly Scots pine for planting between Kingston Hill and Ladderstile Gate) were received from the New Forest.[31] The

The Head Keeper's Lodge (now Bog Lodge) in the nineteenth century by
J. de Koster

A Richmond Park oak in its prime

An oak nearing the end of a long life, but still offering a valuable habitat
to the Park fauna

greater proportion of the trees planted were oak; not only are they the natural tree of the park but also their acorns made (and still make) an important contribution to the diet of the deer. Spanish chestnut were also planted in some quantity for the same reason. But other species were not neglected, and beech, hornbeam, sycamore, thorn and larch were all represented in the nineteenth-century plantings. Silver birch, the 'lady of the woods', may have been planted too, but it is more likely that the majority of birch trees established naturally.

10

The Park – into the Twentieth Century

For the first several years of his tenure as head keeper, Henry G. Sawyer had few problems, apart from the perennial one of providing a sufficient supply of venison for the royal warrant. Then, at the end of September 1886, disaster struck. The unusual behaviour of some fallow deer near Sheen Gate, together with the discovery of a fallow carcass in the vicinity, warned the keepers that something was seriously amiss. But what? The Agricultural Department of the Privy Council Office (predecessor of today's Ministry of Agriculture, Food and Fisheries) was consulted, and they sent their Chief Inspector, A. C. Cope, and Professor V. Horsley of the Brown Institute, London, to investigate.

Cope and Horsley were able to establish the presence of rabies, apparently the first *authenticated* outbreak of rabies among deer in the United Kingdom.[1] In their official report of the Richmond Park outbreak,[2] Cope and Horsley conjectured that 'the distemper' which had destroyed a large number of deer in Cassiobury Park (Herts.) in 1798 and 'which remained so long in Windsor Great Park' may well have been rabies, which is interesting because Henry Sawyer, deer-keeper at Petworth Park (Sussex) in the late eighteenth century, in a letter to his nephew James Sawyer (the first of the Richmond Park Sawyers, and Henry G. Sawyer's grandfather) dated 25 February 1798,[3] refers to both outbreaks. 'I am sorry', he wrote, 'to hear that the distemper has destroyed so many deer at Cassiobury Park and that it should remain so long in Windsor Great Park but I have not the least opinion that the sheep is the cause of it . . .' He then describes a similar outbreak of 'distemper' in Windsor Little Park, where he had probably worked earlier in his life (his father, John Sawyer, who died in 1732, was keeper of the King's Little Park at Windsor early in the eighteenth century), in this instance blaming 'bad weeds' growing in cold, wet land in the north part of that park, for causing the outbreak.

Henry Sawyer had discussed the Windsor Park 'distemper' in an earlier letter to his nephew:[4] 'I never heard of exactly the same disorder among the deer as rages at Windsor Park, but some years past we had a disorder here [Petworth] among the deer, of which so many died or in consequence of which were killed, that I believe we had not above 30 left.' But the Petworth 'disorder' was unlikely to have been rabies. Although the symptoms shown by affected deer, as described by Sawyer, were in some respects similar to Cope and Horsley's description of the rabid Richmond Park deer, there was one major exception. Sawyer specifically stated that, 'They [the deer] never offered to bite each other nor do harm to other animals . . .' whereas in Richmond Park they did. Indeed, this was one of the major findings of the Cope and Horsley investigation, for they were able to prove conclusively that the rabies virus was transmitted by diseased deer attacking and biting healthy animals, something about which there had previously been considerable doubt, with reference not only to deer but to herbivores as a whole.

The disease spread slowly throughout the herd during the winter of 1886–7, and by April 160 animals had died. At first, the greater mortality was among the does and fawns, because the bucks were able to fend off attack from rabid animals with their antlers. After they had shed their antlers, and when in velvet, the bucks proved to be just as vulnerable as the does and fawns. By September the outbreak had been brought under control, by which time 264 fallow had been lost, either dying of the disease or having been shot because they displayed the symptoms.

The outbreak was contained in one area of the park – in the vicinity of Sheen Gate – because of the fallow deer's habit of remaining relatively static, in herds of about one or two hundred, in specific localities. Only the one herd had been decimated; outbreaks of the disease had occurred in an adjacent herd, but by confining this second herd in hastily constructed paddocks and by shooting any animal which showed symptoms (a method of control advocated by Henry Sawyer in 1795), Cope and Horsley were able to prevent further contagion. One final experiment completed their investigation. Four red deer were paddocked on pastures which had been grazed by rabid fallow. The red deer were given their freedom after a period of some months, during which they remained perfectly healthy, thus proving to the satisfaction of the two scientists that the rabies virus could not be spread via contaminated pastures.

Henry G. Sawyer was to report another epidemic, of a much less dramatic nature, eleven years later.[5] Although only sixty to seventy deer were carried off by this epidemic, it is nevertheless of interest. Not only does Sawyer's report of the outbreak describe some of the management practices of the period; it also provides indication of the condition of the atmosphere of the London region at the end of the nineteenth century.

Smog! Smoke had been a London problem for many years, and as early as 1718 it was sufficiently serious to have prompted an official enquiry. In December 1873, during a period of prolonged fog, some of the prize stock at the Islington Cattle Show were suffocated, and others suffered so severely that they had to be slaughtered.[6]

Following a succession of foggy weeks in late November and December 1897, a number of fallow deer, apparently otherwise in good condition, were found dead. A post-mortem, carried out by the head keeper, revealed that the beast's intestines were inflamed, and in most cases the livers congested, but not the respiratory system. At the same time many deer were 'attacked with scour' (diarrhoea) which, according to Sawyer, was 'not uncommon among the deer in Spring when grass is early and white frosts occur but it is unusual to have scour in Autumn or early Winter'. The deaths continued into the new year, and between Christmas and mid-February twelve bucks, ten does and thirty-four fawns were lost. Many of the latter died of weakness, showing no signs of scour, and Sawyer attributed the greater loss of fawns to cessation of lactation by affected does (some does are in fact dry – that is, without milk – as early as late October/November, but most are still lactating well into the New Year).[7]

The head keeper was cautious in his diagnosis of the cause of the outbreak. 'Whether the epidemic is identical with influenza or not it appears to be caused by atmospheric influence – the large deposit of London smoke on the grass during the foggy weather may have proved an irritant,' he explained in his report. He added that many hares had died in the park during the same period and that they displayed symptoms similar to those of the afflicted deer. Possibly both deer and hares had been poisoned as a result of grazing on pastures which had been heavily contaminated by deposits from London smoke.

This was not the first instance of an ailment of this nature. In December 1889, when similar weather conditions prevailed, some fifty healthy bucks were reported[5] to have been similarly stricken. They had been promptly paddocked and fed with castor oil in warm gruel (a thin soup made by boiling oatmeal in water), powdered ginger and 'lamb food', oats and bran. All but five or six recovered, apparently as a result of the treatment. Why the same treatment had not been attempted during the later outbreak is not explained – perhaps it was much more extensive – instead Sawyer fed the herds with beans soaked in turpentine, which he claimed had 'a good and marked effect' – an interesting choice of medication in view of the congested livers. Whitaker,[8] writing in 1892, recommended the spreading of 'Scotch fir' (presumably Scots pine) and spruce boughs, because of their turpentine content, for the control of liver fluke (a parasite which attacks the livers of many herbivores, particularly those which are obliged to pasture on wet land, because the intermediary hosts of the liver fluke are a species of snail which requires a damp habitat).

The losses caused by the two epidemics were never to be made good. Prior to the rabies outbreak there were more than fourteen hundred fallow in the park; by the end of the century there were just over a thousand. However, numbers were no longer so important. By this time it had been realized that the remaining fallow herds of the royal parks were just not sufficiently large to maintain the supply of venison required to satisfy the needs of the Royal Venison Warrant. So measures were taken to reduce the huge quantities of venison which had been called for earlier in the century. Some recipients were unfortunate enough to lose their entitlement altogether. Others found that the amount of venison they were accustomed to receive each season was reduced. Even the royal table suffered, and Queen Victoria agreed to accept a lesser number of carcasses in 1885, and again in 1893.[9] No longer was it necessary to strive to keep the park herds at maximum strength, and the intensive management practices which had been followed for much of the century were gradually eased.

The tradition of supplying stags from Richmond Park for the Royal Hunt continued throughout the reign of Queen Victoria, and a contemporary author describes a 'catch up' of stags in January 1894[10] which indicates that the method used was very similar to that recorded by Edward Jesse sixty years earlier. He also relates an incident which will be of interest to those who walk their dogs in the park today. One day, in early summer, a carriage was making its way from White Lodge to Robin Hood Gate, accompanied by a collie dog, trotting along behind it. The carriage must have passed by a new-born calf hidden close to the carriageway, because a watchful hind attacked, and lightly wounded, the unsuspecting dog, striking at it with her fore-feet. Using the undoubted intelligence of her breed, the collie immediately sought refuge under the still moving carriage, and remained under its protection until the vehicle left the park by Robin Hood Gate. The hind, her protective instincts fully aroused, followed closely behind until it did so.[11]

By the end of the century, most of the large plantations were well established, and the pace of the tree-planting programme, so enthusiastically initiated by Lord Sidmouth, had slackened. The establishment of new plantations was confined to smaller plantings commemorating royal occasions, the first being the Jubilee Plantation at the west end of Queen's Ride, in 1887. This was followed by the first Coronation Plantation, in the south-west of the park, planted in 1902.[12]

The year 1904 was destined to be important in the history of Richmond Park, for it marked the end of the second phase of its history, and the birth

A view near Richmond Gate

of the third, still extant, era. In March of that year George, Duke of Cambridge, Ranger for the past forty-seven years, died, and King Edward VII (1901–10) took into his own hands the rangership (he was also Ranger of St James's and Hyde Park). The King was not unfamiliar with the park, although his first experience of it was probably not the happiest of his life. In April 1858 the seventeen-year-old Prince of Wales had been dispatched to White Lodge, there to be kept 'away from the world' for some months to continue his education and to be taught that which was considered necessary to turn him into the 'first gentleman of the country'. The books which his tutors insisted that he read did not take his interest, and he found the dinner parties arranged for him, at which he was expected to converse with local dignitaries such as Lord John Russell and Professor Richard Owen, hard work.[13] He visited the park again occasionally during 1867–8, staying at White Lodge, before Queen Victoria presented it to the Duke and Duchess of Teck in 1869.

On 25 March 1904 the King was pleased 'to command that steps be taken to render all parts of Richmond Park more accessible to the Public than heretofore. With this object his Majesty has given directions that the preservation of game in the Park shall be discontinued and that woods hitherto closed shall be thrown open where possible without injury to the timber or without detriment to the preservation of order in the Park.'[14] An immediate result was the slaughter of almost 2,500 rabbits, because, being game, they were no longer protected, and this in turn improved the pastures to the benefit of the deer and gave rise to the establishment of many thousands of silver birch seedlings in the enclosed plantations,[15] not all of which were to remain closed: some forty hectares were opened up as a result of the royal command, and two years later a driftway bisecting Sidmouth Plantation was opened to the public.

The King also instructed that 'the administration of the Park should fall on the Office of Works in a greater degree than heretofore'. The appointment was confirmed of the Deputy Ranger, Rear-Admiral Sir A. A. F. Fitz-George (son of the second Duke of Cambridge), who had first taken office in 1898. However, when His Majesty signed the appropriate Warrant on 1 May 1904, he added, 'I have signed the Warrants but hope that the two Deputy Rangers [the second being the Deputy Ranger of St James and Hyde Parks] fully understand that they can give no orders without my permission and any suggestion by them for the well being of the Park shall be submitted to me through the First Commissioner of His Majesty's Works etc.' Edward VII retained the rangership until his death in 1910, but after his initial actions, he was content to allow the First Commissioner and the Office of Works to manage the park. It was his intention that the office of Ranger be abolished, and that that of the Deputy Ranger should lapse on the demise of Fitz-George, who was to outlive the King by twelve years.[16] Thus two ancient offices came to an end.

With the Office of Works accepting responsibility for the administration of the park as a whole came the amalgamation of the departments of the Ranger and the park bailiff, and the creation of a new post, that of the park superintendent. The Deputy Ranger was henceforth to have little active involvement in the affairs of the park, and the Superintendent in effect became the manager, directly responsible to the Office of Works for the day-to-day management of the park. The old-established posts of head keeper and park bailiff were abolished, and the Superintendent was provided with an assistant. The under keeper posts were also abolished, on the grounds that game was no longer to be preserved, and in their place two gamekeepers were appointed to care for the deer herds and for vermin control.

On 1 July 1904 the last of a long line of head keepers, Henry G. Sawyer, was retired. This was the end of a family association which had survived for well over a century and which had produced three generations of head keepers. The first Superintendent was Mr S. Pullman, who had been employed in the park for a number of years in the park bailiff's department as foreman. Benjamin Wells, who had been Henry Sawyer's assistant, was appointed assistant to Pullman. Two of the three gamekeepers were retained, George Wells and Earnest Buckley (it is not clear if Benjamin and George Wells were related, but this could have been the case. The name Wells first appears in park records in March 1876, when a William Wells was employed as a labourer).[17]

Towards the end of the nineteenth century there was mounting public criticism of the practice of hunting the carted stag, and particularly of the royal connection with the sport through the Royal Hunt. In view of this Edward VII, when he came to the throne, decided that it would be expedient to disband the Royal Hunt, despite its long and illustrious history. As a consequence, the number of red deer in the park, which had remained constant at between fifty and sixty throughout the nineteenth century because some were regularly sent to the Royal Hunt paddocks, had leapt to seventy-five by 1906.[18] Edward was himself not averse to field sports, especially shooting, and it is possible that the same public criticism may have had some influence on his decision to discontinue the preservation of game for sport in Richmond Park.

Nor was the King averse to an occasional haunch of red deer venison. It had evidently been customary to send him, when he was Prince of Wales, the haunches of a Richmond Park stag on his birthday – this was over and above the venison supplied for the royal table through the medium of the Royal Venison Warrant. In October 1904 Pullman wrote to the Office of Works[19] enquiring if the haunches should be sent as usual that year, the

King's birthday being in November. In his letter the Superintendent referred to the haunches of 'a stag or heaviour', it having been the custom to provide this venison from a stag which had been castrated (as a calf) for this specific purpose. This caused some confusion at the Office of Works; in 1899 Queen Victoria had commanded that the practice of supplying heaviour venison for the royal table should be 'for ever discontinued' (Chapter 3); however, the haunches *were* sent to the King at Sandringham that year, and thereafter until 1909, when the Lord Steward informed the Office of Works that His Majesty no longer required them.[20] It is not recorded whether or not the stags from which the venison had been taken during the interim years were castrated animals!

On one occasion the King required haunches of red deer from the park to be distributed to various recipients who did not normally receive venison by royal warrant. In 1908 he approved the killing of three stags for this purpose, and, amongst others, haunches were sent to the officers of the Convalescent Home at Osborne (Isle of Wight), the King Edward VII Hospital for Officers, and the Officers' Mess, HM Royal Yacht *Victoria and Albert*. The park staff were not forgotten; His Majesty instructed that the remainder of the carcasses were to be divided between the park staff![21]

'Change' is perhaps not the right word to describe the progress of Richmond Park during the nineteenth century – 'development' is more accurate, in the sense that the park had been brought to a more advanced or highly organized state, in response to the demands made of it. Because there had been no fundamental change; the basic structure remained virtually unaltered. Admittedly the reasons for the park's continuing existence had changed – by 1904 it was no longer a hunting ground; but the change of use had little or no impact on its structure and character. It was still a deer park. It was still made up of varying, and informally bounded, areas of 'wasteland' (land of little or no value for agriculture or silviculture), pastures and 'launds', and woodland not intended for commercial timber production, whose proportions were influenced more by natural restrictions than by man's direction, although he had tried hard to alter them for his own advantage. Witness the land drainage schemes of the 1860s, which had undoubtedly improved the pastures but which had little effect on the wasteland, and the large-scale planting of trees, restricted mainly to higher, better-quality land, which probably did little

Left: Henry G. Sawyer

141

more than replace the trees lost since the enclosure. The creation of the enclosed plantations was not out of character with the medieval deer park, for they, too, had their enclosures, albeit for differing reasons. Relatively large numbers of old, mature oaks, many of them 'stag-headed', still survived to contribute to the impression of ancient parkland. That other feature of the medieval deer park, the fishpond, remained evident in the shape of the Pen Ponds; fish were no longer being 'cropped' from the ponds by the end of the century, but they were still fishponds, not utilized for other purposes.

The Park – the Early Twentieth Century

While the red deer herd continued to flourish during the early years of the twentieth century, the fallow herds were not prospering. Perhaps the intensive management of the nineteenth century, combined with the trauma of the rabies outbreak and the subsequent 'epidemic', had been too much for them. The continuing policy of maintaining more bucks than does could also have been contributory. Whatever the reason, the size of the herds reduced rapidly, and mortality among the fawns was high – of the eighty-five born in the summer of 1905, only fifteen survived their first winter.[1]

Something had to be done to stop the accelerating deterioration, and it was decided to introduce a number of bucks from elsewhere,[2] most of which were supplied by a Mr Richard Porter, who was apparently a professional dealer. He was associated with several transactions involving live deer and the royal parks between 1899 and 1916. For some time he had the use of a paddock in Bushy Park, presumably as temporary accommodation for deer in transit, because in early 1908 two hinds belonging to him escaped from it![3] His first business deal with Richmond Park was in 1906, when he supplied twelve bucks; two years later he was to provide a further ten. Porter was paid not in cash but in kind: one red deer, either a stag or a hind, for each buck safely delivered to the park. Herein lies a hint of intrigue.

Only a few years had passed since Edward VII had disbanded the Royal Hunt on account of adverse public criticism. And even more recently the King had decreed that game should no longer be preserved for sport in Richmond Park. In 1910 a Captain McTaggard bought six hinds from the park, and two years later another six. In 1912 a Mr Headington bought one stag and exchanged another, and four hinds were sold to a Mr Winch.[2] It seems more than coincidental that a Mr G. B. Winch was Master of the Mid-Kent Staghounds between 1903 and 1913, that

A London Underground poster from 1913, by T. Sarg

Messrs F. W. and A. H. Headington were joint Masters of the Berkshire and Buckinghamshire Farmers' Staghounds from 1907 to 1914, and Captain McTaggard Master of the Surrey Staghounds from 1901 to 1915. All these hunted the carted stag.[4] Porter obviously had a ready market for live red deer when he first started to deal with the park. A clue as to what that market was lies in the sale of deer to the various hunts. The connection is further strengthened by a cash deal between Porter and the park in 1913, when he bought ten stags (at £4. 10s. 0d. each) and six hinds (at £3. 10s. 0d. each). There was a strict condition to the sale – the deer were on no account to be resold for sporting purposes![5] Tenuous though it was, a link between the park and deer-hunting still survived.

The Surrey Staghounds paddocked their deer in Carlshalton Park (Surrey) until 1908. There was also in this park a small herd of fallow deer.[6] Possibly this was the source of the bucks supplied by Porter in 1906 and 1908.

Whether as a result of the introduction of new stock, the lesser number of deer in the park, or a combination of both factors, the health of the fallow herds began to improve. It was agreed that the strength of the fallow herd should remain at about eight hundred animals, and it soon became apparent that, in order to maintain this number, more deer than were required for royal warrant purposes would have to be culled. In 1911, for the first time (at least officially!), Richmond Park venison was sold in the marketplace, dressed carcasses fetching 5d. a pound.[2] Three years earlier, on 29 November 1908, another 'first' had been recorded: a buck was knocked down and killed by a motor car.[7]

In 1906 an attempt was made to establish a roe deer colony. In March of that year five roe deer from Lord Ilchester's estates of Milton Abbas (Dorset) were released in Sawpits Plantation, on the edge of Queen's Ride (the plantation was then fenced). Four died almost immediately, but the fifth survived for some time. Coryn de Vere, whose *Handbook of Richmond Park* was published in 1909,[8] observed that one roe, and sometimes more, was frequently to be seen in the plantation. Perhaps the surviving animal was a doe and had produced kids since being released, thus accounting for the occasional sighting of more than one. In April 1910 two more roe – significantly both bucks – were released into the plantation, the supplier again being Lord Ilchester.[9] The attempt was to prove unsuccessful, and a report of 1912[10] records that, 'The last roe deer has not been seen for months.'

During the later years of the nineteenth century there were signs that public access to the park was becoming less restricted. In 1894 Bog (or Queen's) Gate (originally opened in 1736 to provide a private entrance for the royal family on their way to and from White Lodge) was opened to the public for twenty-four hours a day. A new gate was made to facilitate easier access (to foot traffic only). This was probably the first of the now familiar iron 'cradle' gates, which allow unhindered pedestrian use but do not offer the deer an opportunity to wander through. Two years later, in response to public demand, a second cradle gate was constructed adjacent to Bishop's Lodge, but, unlike Bog Gate, Bishop's Gate was locked at night, a circumstance which was to persist for a few more decades. A new cradle gate at Ladderstile, already a public entrance for pedestrians, was built in 1901.[11]

As a direct result of the King's command of 1904, several of the then fenced plantations were thrown open to the park visitor, among them Conduit Wood in 1905 and Sheen Wood a year later. In the same year the 'driftway', which bisects Sidmouth Plantation east to west, was opened to the public during the summer months. The systematic creation of new plantations continued, albeit on a more modest scale than in the previous century. The first of the Coronation Plantations, beside Dann's Pond (named after Alfred Dann, a gamekeeper in the 1870s) and only recently unfenced, was planted in 1902 to commemorate the coronation of Edward VII; Teck Plantation (named after the Duke and Duchess of Teck, who occupied White Lodge between 1869 and 1899), the still enclosed wood immediately to the west of Sheen car-park, dates from 1905.[12]

Apart from its providing accommodation for some of Cromwell's soldiers between 1652 and 1658,[13] war had largely passed Richmond Park by – that is, until the First World War (1914–18), during which a large military camp was established on what is now the golf courses, and a fenced-off enclosure, known as the 'bombing compound', which appeared beside the carriageway a hundred metres west of Sheen Cross-roads. A hospital, the South African War Hospital, was built on the parkland between Conduit Wood and Bishop's Lodge, and a second pedestrian gate, Cambrian Gate, was provided specifically to serve this unit. During the War some forty hectares near Sheen Gate were put to the plough, and crops of oats and potatoes grown. Garden allotments, administered by Richmond Borough Council, were sited in the north-west corner.[14] The tradition of renting grazing for cattle persisted, and in 1914 there were 143 head of cattle in the park, some of which belonged to park staff. The grazing was shared not only with deer but with six agricultural horses, two saddle horses and two driving ponies, all of which were used by various members of staff in pursuance of their duties.[15]

The war was also to affect the deer herds. In 1916, to augment worsening meat shortages throughout the country, fifty fallow and twenty-four red deer were slaughtered and sold to the Central Meat Market.[16] There were other reasons which made it desirable to reduce the size of the herds: grazing was restricted by military activity, and grain to supplement the winter diet of the deer was in short supply. The following year more venison was sold to the Central Meat Market, most of which was sent to victual HM ships of the fleet, 'where it has been much appreciated'.[17] Military activity affected the herds in other ways too, and in January 1918 three bucks managed to entangle themselves fatally in the army telephone lines which then festooned the park. By April 1918 there were only 413 fallow and forty-six red deer left.[18] This was, however, not the principle cause which led to the suspension of the Royal Venison Warrant later that year: the Government had been obliged to introduce general food rationing towards the end of the war, and, as official correspondence put it, 'Now that rationing is in force it certainly seems wrong to distribute deer by Warrant . . .'[17]

The warrant was revived in time for the buck season of 1920. Cultivated areas were returned to parkland soon after the cessation of hostilities, including the allotments, which Richmond Borough Council were required to vacate by Lady Day (25 March) 1920. The military camps were quickly dismantled. Only the South African War Hospital, which had by then been taken over by the Ministry of Pensions, survived, but not for long because it too was demolished in 1925. Military use of the park was to linger on for a number of years though. In 1922 some thirty 'Field Days' were held, involving large numbers of troops, and the Household Cavalry, with the Guards Regiments, were regular visitors.[18]

Not surprisingly, the fallow herds were once again in trouble. The disruption of the war years, continuing military activity and a severe winter in 1920–21 reversed the trend of improvement which had been established in the pre-war era. Other factors played a part. Public use of the park increased dramatically after the war – according to one source,[18] a fine Saturday encouraged as many as two thousand motorists to enter by way of Sheen and Roehampton Gates alone. In early summer visitors were picking up new-born fawns, imagining them to be abandoned, and handing them over to the park-keepers (successors to the nineteenth-century park constables, the change of title probably dating from 1904). Though the fawns were returned as soon as possible to the place where they had been found, it was suspected, probably with some justification, that the does did not always return to their offspring.[19]

For the second time within a few years, it was decided that 'a change of blood' might repair the damage. Previously tapped sources were, in the main, no longer available, so the Commissioner of Works, Sir Lionel Earle, wrote to a selection of historic deer-park owners, seeking fallow deer on either a purchase or an exchange basis. 'The public of London', the letter read, 'derive so much pleasure and interest from the deer that it would be a thousand pities if the two surviving herds (Richmond and Bushy Parks) were allowed to degenerate.'[20] There was in fact a third royal park which still carried fallow deer – Windsor Great Park. This park was no longer administered by the Office of Works, having been returned to the Office of Woods and Forests in the latter part of the previous century (in 1924 the Office of Woods etc. became the Office of the Commissioners of Crown Lands). There were also fallow deer in Greenwich Park, where a limited number were paddocked (a small number of paddocked fallow deer are still kept there, a reminder that Greenwich, like most royal parks, past and present, originated as a deer park).

There was good response to Sir Lionel's plea for assistance, and over the next five years fallow deer were sent from a number of deer parks, among them Ashridge, Buckinghamshire, Woodhall, Hertfordshire, Wonersh, Surrey and Petworth. Some were purchased, others obtained on an exchange basis, but, unlike the introductions of the previous century, there were only a few gifts. In the latter category were four bucks from the Duke of Buccleugh's Boughton Park.

The Duke was to become personally involved in the affairs of the deer herds of the royal parks. He entered into correspondence with Sir Lionel[21] on the subject of deer-park management, a subject in which he was both knowledgeable and interested – appropriately so: the family has owned the 145-hectare Boughton Park since 1776 (it was a deer park as early as 1528), and the name Buccleugh is itself associated with deer by tradition. It is said that many centuries ago a young Scott (the family name), entered a narrow glen or *cleugh* during a royal hunt and seized the hunted buck as it stood at bay. Throwing the beast across his shoulders, he carried it out of the *cleugh* and presented it to the Scottish monarch. The King, pleased, designated the youthful hunter there and then, as of the 'Buck Cleugh'.[22]

In one of his letters, dated 2 April 1923, the Duke explained that he did not feed the Boughton herd (all fallow) supplementary rations in winter, with the exception of a few acorns and horse chestnuts. He considered the park pasture sufficient to sustain them through the winter but acknowledged that his pasture, being on richer soil, was of better quality than that of Richmond and Bushy Parks. 'But one necessary thing to have good deer is to graze a sufficient number of bullocks to eat the rough grass down,' he wrote. The Duke visited Richmond Park, to see for himself, on at least one occasion, during which he had a long conversation with the park Superintendent, Benjamin Wells, who had succeeded Pullman in 1919. Wells was of the opinion that there had been a degree of mismanagement of the herds in the past few years, an opinion with which the Duke was inclined to agree.

In another letter, Buccleugh recommended that the areas of bracken in the park could be beneficially reduced. He also suggested that the quality of park fallow deer was dependent on the 'dams' and advised Sir Lionel to introduce does rather than bucks – an interesting piece of advice, in view of the policy laid down in 1843 by the Commissioners of HM Woods etc., requiring a ratio of five males to three females to be established in the fallow herds of the royal parks, and advice which did not go unheeded: a number of does were brought in from Ashstead Park, Surrey and Surrenden Park, Kent in 1925.

In the years to follow, there were generally more does than bucks in the herds, a reversal of the trend of previous years. By April 1928[23] there were more than six hundred fallow in the park, and one in three adult does had successfully reared fawns, in contrast to only one in seven in the year 1921–2. For the second time within twenty years a deteriorating situation had been turned round, and the fallow herds were prospering, a situation which was to continue until 1939, when, once again, war intervened.

The Duke of Buccleugh was to be involved in the affairs of the park one more time. In 1929 the Office of Works were considering a proposal to introduce exotic deer species into Richmond Park, and his opinion was sought. Wise counsel prevailed, and the proposal came to naught. Had it been otherwise, the presence of exotic deer, interesting though this may have been, would surely have detracted from the historic character of an English deer park.

There were few problems with the red deer herd, which, during the inter-war years, was maintained at a strength of about a hundred animals. R. W. Lucas, park Superintendent between 1928 and 1931 (it is unlikely that R.W. was related to the Lucases of the eighteen and nineteenth centuries), expressed some concern in 1929, when he complained to the Office of Works that, 'The red deer are not in very good condition and stand in need of new blood in order to eradicate rickets and other diseases due to in-breeding.' The records suggest that Lucas's views were probably more alarmist than factual, because no 'new blood' was introduced until 1938, yet the herds continued to prosper during the 1930s. The 'new blood' came from Warnham Park, renowned for the quality and size of its stags, in the form of a three-year-old stag 'with a fine wide head of 12 points' and two young hinds, in exchange for three Richmond Park hinds.[24]

Red deer continued to be sold from time to time. Of note were the two stags sold to Lord Astor in 1927. Lord Astor shipped the animals to his Ardlussa Lodge estate, on the island of Jura (Inner Hebrides), where they were released with the intention of improving the strain of the indigenous red deer. Unfortunately 'the best-laid schemes o'mice an'men, Gang aft aglay',[25] and Lord Astor's stalker – a man named MacKay who had many years experience and was highly regarded – made the dramatic mistake of shooting one of the stags within a year of its release, despite the fact that one ear of each stag had been suitably nicked to aid identification on the hill![26] In 1930 two stags were sent to Raby Castle Park (Co. Durham), an ancient deer park which still contains both red and fallow herds. According to one source, red deer were still being sold to hunts, specifically the Norwich Staghounds (the last hunt in England to hunt the carted stag, the sport finally coming to an end in 1963). And in December 1930 six hinds were sold to a Mr Walls (for £3. 10s. 0d. each). It may, or may not, be coincidental that the Master of the Sussex Staghounds, a hunt which was in being for only the brief period 1930–31, was a Mr Tom Walls![27]

By 1915 a new land use had become evident in the park: a block of football pitches had been established west of Bog Gate, and a cricket pitch occupied open ground between Thatched House Lodge and Ladderstile Gate.[28] Between the wars the number of winter games pitches was to proliferate, and they occupied virtually all level areas of parkland of sufficient area throughout the park. Another kind of sports facility was opened on the east side of the Beverley Brook – that area of the park which had never been open to public access, then known as the Crown Meadows or Great Paddocks.

The idea of constructing a golf course in the park was first raised in 1921. Golfing facilities for the 'artisan' class, who were unable to afford membership of the several private clubs in the vicinity, were practically non-existent in south-west London, and Lord Riddell, first Baron of Walton Heath and President of the Artisan Golfers Association, enthusiastically took up the plight of the local artisans. He formed a consortium comprising local businessmen and dignitaries, who came to the conclusion that the most suitable site for an artisans' golf course was in Richmond Park. The proposal instigated considerable public debate, and the correspondence columns of newspapers, both national and local, were crowded with letters arguing the pros and cons. Eventually agreement was reached between the consortium and the Office of Works: the consortium agreed to fund the capital costs and to undertake financial responsibility for the future management of the course in such a way that green fees would be kept to a level which the artisan classes would find acceptable. The course was to be open to any member of the public who wished to play golf, providing, of course, that the appropriate fee was paid. When the proposal was put before George V for royal assent, he was at first not greatly taken with it, but he gave his consent when he realized that the project would be to the benefit of those who could not otherwise afford to play golf.

The course was designed and built by J. H. Taylor, a prominent golfer of the period, and F. Hawtree. That the enterprise had full royal support became evident on 9 June 1923, when the Prince of Wales (the late Duke of Windsor, who was born in White Lodge, Richmond Park, in 1894) officially opened the course by driving off the first tee. The ceremony was further marked by the Prince presenting a gold sovereign to the spectator

THE FIRST MUNICIPAL LINKS NEAR TOWN: RICHMOND GOLF COURSE.

A Pictorial Diagram Drawn Specially for "The Illustrated London News" by W. B. Robinson.

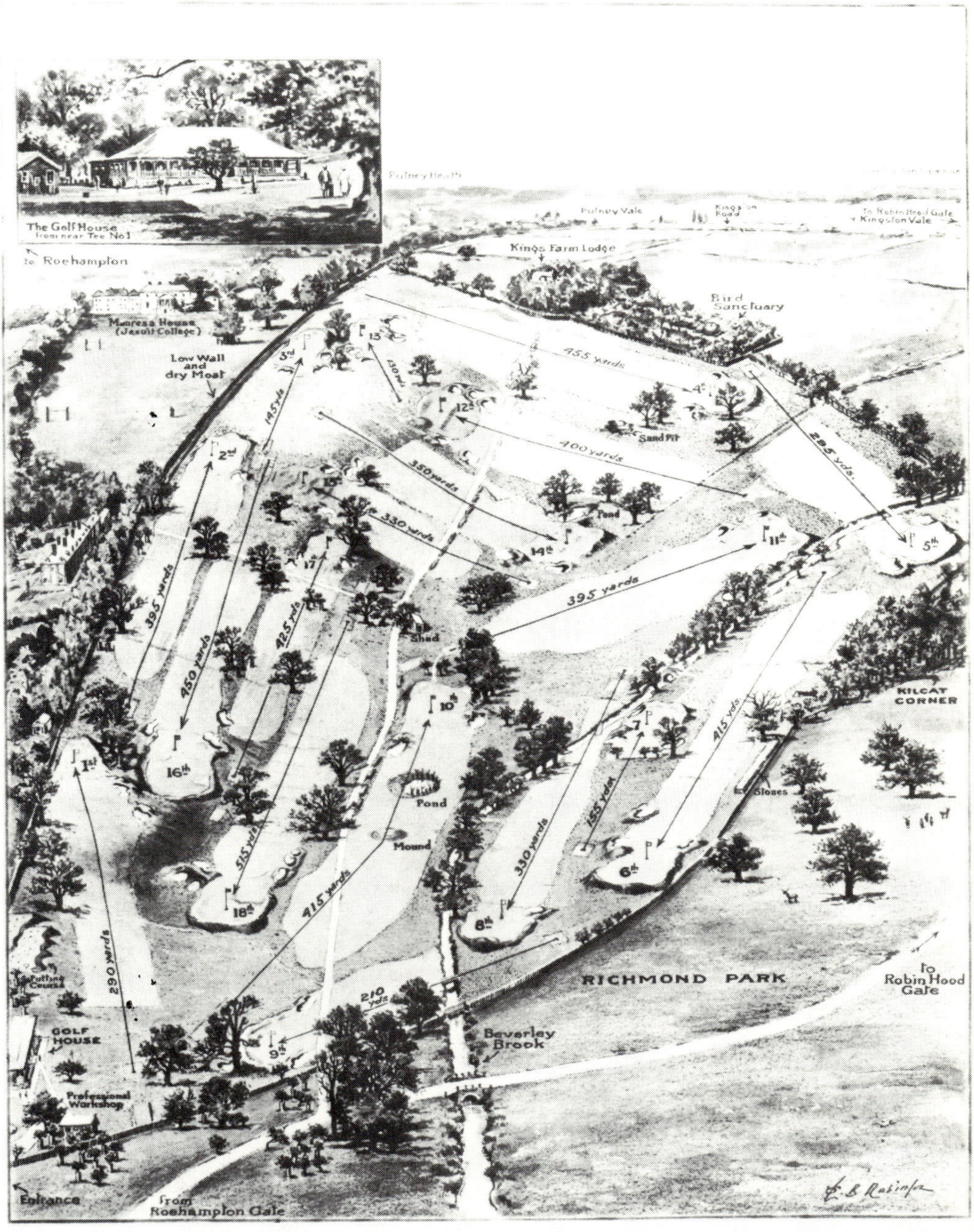

The Golf House from near Tee No 1
Putney Heath
Putney Vale
Kingston Road
To Robin Hood Gate & Kingston Vale
to Roehampton
Kings Farm Lodge
Manresa House (Jesuit College)
Low Wall and dry Moat
Bird Sanctuary
455 yards
4th
3rd
145 yds
13
150 yds
12th
Sand Pit
400 yards
2nd
295 yds.
15th
350 yards
330 yds
Pond
14th
11th
5th
17
395 yards
395 yards
Shed
425 yds
450 yards
10th
KILCAT CORNER
16th
7
155 yds
415 yds
Pond
Mound
330 yards
6th
515 yds
18th
415 yards
8th
290 yards
RICHMOND PARK
To Robin Hood Gate
Putting Course
210 yds
GOLF HOUSE
9th
Beverley Brook
Professional Workshop
Entrance
from Roehampton Gate

WHERE ARTISANS AND ROYALTY ARE EQUALLY WELCOME: THE 1s. 6d.-A-ROUND RICHMOND PARK COURSE.

The Municipal Golf Course, 1923

The Duke of Windsor (then Prince of Wales) opens the Prince's Golf Course, June 1923. J. H. Taylor holds aloft the traditional golden guinea.

who retrieved and returned the ball to him. Two years later a second eighteen-hole course was opened, such was the success of the venture. On this occasion the Duke of York (later George VI), who spent the early years of his married life at White Lodge, executed the ceremonial drive. The recipient of the customary gold sovereign on this occasion had to work harder than his predecessor, because the Duke reputedly sent the ball some 150 metres down the fairway, in contrast to the Prince's modest thirty metres! Not surprisingly, the first course is known as 'the Prince's' and the second as 'the Duke's'![29]

In 1927 the Office of Works bought out the consortium, by agreement, and accepted responsibility for the management of the courses.[30] Today the Department of the Environment, successor to the Office of Works, still holds responsibility, and they are maintained as public golf courses, financed from the revenue generated by the golf played on them.

Early in the 1930s a somewhat incongruous structure was to appear in the park, near Richmond Gate. This was a replica of a Victorian bandstand, and in pre-war years summer Sunday afternoon band concerts held there were a popular attraction. The concerts were re-introduced after the war but did not have the same appeal, and the bandstand fell into disuse in the mid 1950s.[31] It was eventually dismantled for re-erection in the much more appropriate setting of Regent's Park, in 1975. A group of twenty-five silver birch, planted in 1977 to commemorate the Silver Jubilee of HM the Queen, now flourish on the site.

By 1939 Richmond Park had truly become a public park, just as its last Ranger, Edward VII, had intended. Despite the huge increase in public use, its character and tradition had not been destroyed. Not only was it important as a deer park and a place of public recreation: it had become an oasis of wild life, an area of historic parkland of sufficient size to hold a varied and wide-ranging ecosystem. There was perhaps a faint cloud on the horizon – a trace of Victorian municipal park design creeping in, in the form of formal outdoor sports facilities and the bandstand. The events of the next few years were, however, to have a dramatic effect on the park, just as they had over all of Europe, and indeed much of the world.

Left: The Tea Terrace, Pembroke Lodge Gardens

12

The Park of Today

The World War of 1939–45 disrupted Richmond Park to a greater degree than any other event in its three-hundred-year history. Most of the pastures were put to the plough, the agricultural operations being under the control of the County of Surrey War Agricultural Executive Committee. A military encampment involving large numbers of semi-permanent buildings and huts, occupied a twenty-hectare site on the plateau in the south-west of the park.[1] Anti-aircraft gun batteries were located in strategic positions. A 'sterilizing pit', used for bleeding explosives from unexploded enemy bombs dropped on London, lay between Ham Cross and Isabella Plantation. The Pen Ponds were drained and camouflaged to prevent their use as a navigational aid by enemy aircraft.

Public access was restricted. Routine maintenance work suffered, and tree planting was more or less abandoned.[2] In early 1941 the Office of Works decided that the deer herds should be reduced to 150; by December 1942 there were, according to official records, only a hundred left. In an effort to prevent crop damage, an attempt was made to drive the remaining animals into Petersham Park (one of the few areas not touched by war) and to confine them there with electric fencing. But the attempt failed, and in the spring of 1943 the Agricultural Executive Committee proposed that the deer herds should be disposed of altogether. The proposal came to nought, although the herds continued to dwindle during the summer, to reach an all-time low of sixty-eight fallow and thirteen red, which had to share what remained of the grazing (some 140 hectares of the park was then under cultivation) with a flock of 350 sheep, and fifty head of cattle. Despite the limited pastures, and the competition from domestic stock, the deer apparently flourished, for that same summer the park Superintendent (Mr A. E. Wilson. 1931–51) reported that, 'Our present stock [of deer] is much more virile and healthy than the deer which were here in 1931 when I took charge.'[3]

The end of a Hermann. The bomb sterilizing pit used during the 1939–45 war

The north of the Park from the air, 1948. Robin Hood Gate, the Pen Ponds,
Queen's Ride and Sidmouth Plantation can be easily identified, as can the areas
of the Park then under arable cultivation

By 1946 both red and fallow deer were increasing in number, albeit slowly. During the next three years the red deer continued their progress, but apparently not the fallow. Official records tell of a series of unspecified accidents which had reduced their numbers to only fifty by the end of 1949. However, the same source records that, just twelve months later, there were 179 of them! It was during this period that work started in putting to rights the ravages of war, and one of the first tasks tackled was the repair of the fencing of the plantations. Before that, the plantations were driven through, and it only then became evident that a goodly number of fallow had sought war-time refuge in the safety of the undergrowth of the larger plantations.

Richmond was not the only royal park which had been sacrificed, on a temporary basis, to the war effort, nor was it only the London parks that were affected. Much of the Great Park at Windsor had been turned over to agriculture early in the War and was to remain as arable land long after the cultivated sections of Richmond had been returned to parkland. A small herd of deer had been maintained, in the hope that they might, one day, again have the freedom of the park. But it was not to be. In 1949 George VI agreed to the dispersal of the remnants of the once great red deer herds of Windsor, which were famed for their fine quality and heavy weight. They have been described as being 'bigger than those in almost any other English Park and owe their great size and magnificent heads to German blood. The German deer were introduced by Charles II after the Civil War and today that gigantic strain still shows in the Windsor herd.'[4] Perhaps it was this factor which prompted Sir Louis Greig* to make formal application to the King for as many red deer as could be spared from the remnants of the Windsor herd, for Richmond Park. The King was pleased to agree to the request, but there was a condition attached: if it was decided to re-introduce deer to the Great Park in the future, he would expect Richmond Park to assist in forming a new herd.[6] The following year twenty-four deer were transferred to Richmond; some also went to the Duke of Beaufort's Badminton Park, Gloucestershire, and others found themselves north of the Border, released into the Balmoral deer forest.[7]

The transformation from farm and military encampment was slow, and it was not until the early 1950s that cultivated areas were returned to parkland. In 1956 the wrought-iron carriage gates at Kingston, opened by

* At the special request of George VI, the office of Deputy Ranger of Richmond Park was revived in 1932 specifically for Group Captain Sir Louis Greig, Gentleman Usher-in-Ordinary to the King. Sir Louis and his family were resident at Thatched House Lodge until his death in 1953, after which his widow remained in residence for a further three years. Although his office was largely a sinecure, Sir Louis took an active interest in the affairs of the Park.[5]

Agriculture in the Park, 1940–50. Ploughing the plateau north of Bog Lodge

Queen Victoria in 1861, had still to be restored, and the temporary wooden gates which had replaced them early in the war, by then in dilapidated condition, remained in position.[8] The buildings associated with the military encampment were not finally demolished until the 1960s, but they served at least one useful peace time purpose in that they were utilized as the Olympic Village for the 1948 Olympic Games.[9]

One of the first moves to return the park to its former glory concerned the trees. The first post-war plantation, Queen Elizabeth Wood, was established in 1948. Three years later, Prince Charles' Spinney, south-east of Isabella Plantation, was planted. Each occupies four hectares.

Since then there have been but two additions to the list of plantations. The 1953 Coronation Plantation, mainly beech, is sited not far from the 1902 Coronation Plantation. Queen Mother's Copse, which lies between White Lodge (now the home of the junior section of the Royal Ballet School) and Roehampton Gate was planted in 1980 to commemorate the Queen Mother's eightieth birthday. The copse consists of eighty English oaks, the first of which was planted by HRH Princess Alexandra and the remainder, many of which were donated by school groups, the Friends of Richmond Park (the amenity society most closely associated with the park) and private individuals.

Although the nineteenth-century tradition of the systematic establishment of plantations has lost much of its impetus, tree-planting continues on a scale sufficient to ensure that there is no reduction in the park's tree stocks. Policy dictates that only indigenous forest trees, or long-established introduced species, be planted, with English oak predominating.[10] As woods slowly decay and parkland gradually takes over where once there were trees, so a recently planted area waits to fill the gap. The landscape is not fixed for all time – it is in a state of fluidity, as it always has been. However, historical features such as Queen's Ride, Hornbeam Walk and the cedars of Petersham Park will hopefully always be preserved.

Two factors stand out above all else in post-war Richmond Park: the first is its remarkable recovery from the ravages of war, without loss of its distinctive and historic character; the second – the establishment of a woodland garden in the west section of the Isabella Plantation.

The area now occupied by this plantation was named 'Isabell Slade' as early as 1771,[11] but no record has yet been discovered which associates a lady of that name with the park. There could be an alternative explanation. The word 'isabel' describes something which is drab or a dingy yellow-grey colour. A 'slade', by definition, is a shallow valley or an area of low-lying, moist ground, conditions which are to be found in the north of the plantation. Here also is to be found weathered clay, capable of producing a drab, yellow colour if stirred up by, for example, deer

The late George Thomson, MVO, beside Thomson's Pond in the Woodland
Garden

Two views of the Woodland Garden, Isabella Plantation

165

wallowing, as is their wont at certain times of the year. This alternative explanation is at least logical, if unromantic!

The origins of the garden are not well recorded. It is said that the original intention, in the late 1940s, was to plant informally along the banks of the only watercourse in the plantation, to create a pleasant woodland walk. The streamside walk grew to its present size largely through the inspiration of the late George Thomson, MVO, a Scottish forester who was park Superintendent from 1951 to 1971, ably assisted by the late Wally Miller, BEM, head gardener until his retirement in 1980. The essence of a woodland garden is informality, and because the Isabella Garden is not of static design – no landscape or garden architect, working to some master plan, was involved – change and development were, and indeed still are, a continuous process, thus allowing the vital natural and informal elements to flourish.

Apart from the topography of the plantation, located as it is on a gentle south-east/north-west slope with just the hint of a shallow valley, the soft, dappled shade filtering through the mature oak canopy, and the typical acid, woodland soil provide ideal conditions for a woodland garden. Rhododendrons, azaleas, magnolia, camellias and many other mainly ericaceous shrubs and plants thrive under such conditions, with heaths and heathers complementing them in one of the two large open spaces in the garden. Planting has been carried out in bold clumps and groups, creating numerous vistas, some blind, other interconnecting and crossing. The overall effect has been enhanced by the creation of a further two streams, which flow roughly parallel to the natural stream, their banks clad with evergreen azaleas, with primulas and other moisture-loving plants along their base. Of the garden's three ponds, only the top one, the Still Pond, is original. The middle pond, in the second of the large open spaces, is appropriately named 'Thomson's Pond'. Peg's Pond, at the bottom of the garden, is the outfall for all the streams, the only one to contain an island, which supports four mature weeping willows. This is Wally's Island. Prior to being taken into the fold of the garden, Peg's Pond was simply a muddy deer wallow in open parkland.[12]

Essentially a spring garden, it is at its most colourful in May, but it has much to offer throughout the year. Although by no means unimportant as a collection of trees, shrubs and plants, it is basically a people's garden, just as George Thomson had intended.

The garden is one of several bird sanctuaries in Richmond Park. The importance of the park as a natural habitat for the indigenous and migrant birds of south-east England was recognized early this century, and for well over fifty years the major enclosed plantations have been designated bird sanctuaries, as have the Pen Ponds. During this time management effort has been directed towards the development of suitable habitats to

Stepping-stones across the stream in the Woodland Garden

attract bird species to the park, rather than introducing them by other means. Hence the absence of the collections of exotic water fowl, which are to be found in most of London's royal parks. An early example of the creation of a habitat, in this instance to attract water fowl, is the reed beds at the head of the Upper Pen Pond. Those were established in the early 1920s, with reeds brought from the Norfolk Broads.[13] A more recent example concerns the planting of a number of small gorse enclosures, on the south side of the park, the hope being that linnets and other small bird species will find them attractive as breeding sites. An added incentive to maintain some proportion of gorse in the flora of the park is the specific mention of this shrub in its early history.

It is for this same reason that, exceptionally, two species of birds are artificially raised for release into the park from time to time. In 1636, when the Marquis of Hamilton reported the arrival of deer 'into these parts' to Charles I (Chapter 4), he also referred to pheasant and partridge flying 'from the New Park to the woods adjoining'.

The flora of the park is such that a wide and varied range of natural habitats is available to bird life. The ancient hollow oaks, for example, provide rich pickings for woodpeckers and tree creepers and offer nesting facilities to a number of species, one of them the mallard duck, which has come to appreciate the advantages of nesting off the ground. Owls enjoy their protection, and some are used as roosting sites for the small Pipistrelle bat, numbers of which can be seen, late on any summer evening. Edward Jesse refers to the discovery of 'vast numbers' of bats under the roof of an old building in the park in the early nineteenth century.[14] A hundred years later another amateur natural historian, C. L. Collenette, was not so optimistic. He recorded that the Pipistrelle could be seen on any summer evening but that he never saw 'more than three or four in the course of one walk'.[15] It is not only birds and bats which are attracted to the old, decaying trees. A recent survey, by staff from the British Natural History Museum, acting on behalf of the Nature Conservancy Council, recorded the presence of more than eight hundred species of beetles, including some which have been found at only one or two other sites, and one which has not been found elsewhere in the country.[16]

One bird habitat which has suffered in recent years is the open grassland. This is due entirely to the greatly increased use of parkland by visitors, and their dogs, and has resulted in the loss of one or two species, notably the woodlark. However, there remains a healthy bird population; in 1976 no fewer than 107 different species of birds were observed, of which sixty successfully bred.[17] This compares favourably with a list of 133 species built up during *several* years of observations by Collenette.[18] Today, some species are present in over-abundant numbers. The carrion crow, which plays havoc with newly hatched mallard ducklings on their journey from nest to water, comes into the park in quantity every day but escapes control measures simply by roosting elsewhere. Every autumn, wood pigeon in their thousands flock in to make the most of the acorn crop, thus depriving the resident fauna of a proportion of its natural food.

Although the Pen Ponds are now primarily bird sanctuaries, their piscatory origins are not ignored. Angling for coarse fish (there are no game fish) is allowed by permit. The ponds are not managed as a fishery, but they are restocked with fish occasionally. Some large carp inhabit the waters but are seldom caught. Pike, some weighing 10 kg, are caught from time to time. Eels are also found in the ponds, and sometimes in the various ditches which empty into the Beverley Brook; they even find their way to Peg's Pond in the Woodland Garden. But it is unlikely that they are as common as they were 150 years ago. Jesse, speculating on the natural history of the eel, talks of the 'very great quantity of young ones which migrate from those ponds [the Pen Ponds] every year', a migration toward the sea which apparently took place 'at nearly the same day in the month of May'. A fisherman as well as a naturalist, the largest eel he caught was one of just over 2 kg from Richmond Park.[19]

The smaller ponds of the park are full of pond life, and one, Ham Dip Pond, is traditionally used as a study area by local schools. Of the amphibians, the common frog is to be found in plenty; there is no shortage of the common toad, and smooth newts inhabit most of the ponds.

Undoubtedly the most destructive of the smaller mammals of the park is that intruder from North America, the grey squirrel. Robber of birds' nests, destroyer of young trees, pillager of the gardeners' bulbs and corms, it can only be regarded as vermin. Grey squirrels were first introduced into Britain between 1890 and 1916, when batches of them were released at different times in several places around London. Early this century, a batch of a hundred were liberated on Kingston Hill, on the south side of the park, by an unknown American.[20] Within twenty years they had become a pest. Although large numbers are now killed every year, satisfactory control is unlikely to be achieved because of the lack of it beyond the boundaries of the park. The red squirrel seems to have been comparatively rare in the park well before the arrival of the grey, and has been absent for the past fifty years or so.

The rabbit. Friend or foe? Certainly, if too abundant, it is a destructive beast, capable of causing immense damage to young trees and crops. Introduced from the Continent in the twelfth century, the conie or rabbit was considered a beast of the warren (hares, foxes, badgers and, for a time,

Overleaf: A family of swans on the upper Pen Pond. *Inset*: Badgers leave the sett

roe deer were others) and therefore outside the protection of the Forest Laws. It nevertheless enjoyed the protection of landowners for several centuries, being valued for its meat and for sport. The rabbit has a historic right to its place in the park, and hopefully will never be eradicated, although control is necessary to prevent its numbers rising to a point at which it can be defined as a pest. The hare, a relative of the rabbit, has, alas, gone from the park, the last one being seen in the mid-1950s. Unlike the rabbit, which has the shelter of its burrow, the hare is surface-dwelling, a creature of open grass and downland. Habitat disturbance was its downfall.

Two other beasts of the warren successfully survive. The badger remains well established, and there are several active setts, some of them probably centuries old, scattered throughout the park. Because badgers are mainly nocturnal in habit, the park visitor will be fortunate to see one. However, in autumn and early winter there is often clear evidence of their presence, in the form of extensive areas of neatly turned back turf. The badger has been seeking the grubs of the daddy-long-legs (leather jackets), which are sometimes to be found in quantity at the base of the sod.

That creature which has, in recent years, so successfully adapted to the suburban environment, the fox, is more likely to be seen by the park visitor who proceeds cautiously in less frequently used areas. Although the fox is also largely nocturnal, cubs may occasionally be seen on a sunny day in early summer, playing near the earth. Few commuters, driving to work through the park between Robin Hood and Roehampton, realize that, every spring before the bracken is fully grown, their progress may be being observed by a vixen, at the entrance to her earth, not two hundred metres from the carriageway. The park fox hunts but little, finding adequate food supplies in the litter bins within its walls, and the dustbins of surrounding suburbia.

The long-established office of mole-catcher was still extant in 1870–1871, during which year it attracted a salary of £20,[21] but it seems to have become redundant shortly afterwards. Jesse's writings suggest that earlier in the nineteenth century moles were relatively common only in limited areas of the park where the soil was loamy (and, therefore, well populated with earthworms, a basic item of the mole's diet).[22] Collenette describes moles as being rare and by the 1930s absent altogether from open parkland.[23] They are no longer found anywhere in the park. Another animal which is partial to the odd earthworm is the hedgehog. It was probably never very common in the park, but it is still occasionally found in some of the lodge gardens and may be resident in one or two of the older plantations.

By and large, the deer herds have prospered in the last thirty years, although a few minor setbacks have been experienced. During 1964–5 a poor crop of fawns was produced, and examination of culled fallow carcasses later in the year showed a high incidence of abscess in the lungs and livers. Suspicion fell on the silage which was then fed to the herds to supplement their winter diet and when the silage was replaced with a mixture of locust beans, corn and maize the following winter, the health of the herd immediately began to improve.

The red deer were apparently not affected, which was perhaps just as well because they had another disorder to contend with. Isolated cases of 'staggers' (*enzootic ataxia*), similar to 'swayback' in sheep, had occurred from time to time (the 'rickets' which R. W. Lucas complained of in 1929 was probably staggers), but in the three years following 1964 the number of cases of this irreversible disease accelerated. The condition is not yet fully understood; it involves a progressive weakness and lack of co-ordination of the hind quarters (hence the name 'staggers'), resulting from degenerative changes in the spinal column, and appears to be associated with the affected animal's failure to assimilate the trace element copper from its food. For reasons which so far defy explanation, the 'outbreak' died down, and since then isolated cases have occurred at intervals of twelve to eighteen months. Curiously, the disorder seems to affect only park red deer, suggesting the possibility of a genetic factor, and a case is yet to be confirmed in wild deer.

It was for this reason that, when HM the Queen and Prince Philip, Ranger of Windsor Great Park, decided to re-introduce red deer into that park in 1978, the stock came from the red deer of Balmoral Forest. Later a single stag joined them from Glen Feshie, a gift to the Prince of Wales from the British Deer Society, of which the Prince is patron, and another was acquired from Glenmazeran. It is interesting to compare the beasts of this now well-established herd with those from other deer parks. Although they have thrived on the richer pastures of their new habitat, the Windsor deer retain the shorter, stockier body of the red deer from the hill.

So Richmond Park red deer herd did not return to Windsor, as George VI had envisaged. However, seven did set out on a much longer journey that same year. Two stags and five hinds crossed the Atlantic, by air, to the Upper Clements Wild Life Park, on the north-west coast of Nova Scotia, a Silver Jubilee gift from HM the Queen to the people of that province of Canada. Although this nucleus of a red deer herd did not leave the park until 1978, the gift was marked in Silver Jubilee year by the presentation of a warrant authorizing the gift. That Richmond Park deer were chosen was appropriate. Nine years earlier, the Government of Ontario had presented the people of Great Britain with a hundred Canadian sugar maples to mark the centenary of Ontario's first official representation in the

United Kingdom. The maples were planted in Richmond Park, on the hillside above Gallows Pond, near Kingston Gate, where they now flourish. It is unfortunate that autumn temperatures in this country do not fall sufficiently low to bring out the best of the autumn leaf tints for which the Canadian maple is so well known.

Despite an acquaintanceship of almost a century, the deer and the motor vehicle are not quite compatible. Every year a number of deer die on the park carriageways, victims of car accidents. Speed, on the part of the vehicle (as early as 1908 Mr W. Heaton Armstrong MP was fined £4 and costs for exceeding the 20 mph limit)[24] and careless driving are, without doubt, responsible for some of the accidents – but not all: sometimes a dog, out of control, will chase deer across the carriageway in front of a passing vehicle, with disastrous results. In order to assist both the driver and deer, a twenty-metre-wide strip of grassland on each side of the carriageway is kept mown to create a 'visibility zone'.

On two occasions since the war, the park carriageways have been open to public traffic after dark. During the winter of 1961–2 the gates were kept open until 8 p.m. in an attempt to ease 'rush hour' traffic congestion. So many deer were killed on the park roads between sunset and park closing time that this trial was quickly abandoned. For an eighteen month period in 1979–80, the carriageway between Kingston and Richmond was kept open to traffic until midnight, on account of a major road closure outside the west boundary of the park. Despite experiments with a number of aids designed to discourage deer from approaching the carriageway, there was again a dramatic increase in the number of deer killed and injured on the road. On this occasion many of the victims were bucks – so many that the balance of the fallow herds was seriously affected, an imbalance which has only recently been corrected.

Here is one of the three major factors which determine at what strength the deer herds should be maintained. There must be sufficient insurance, by way of numbers, to give the herds reasonable opportunity of recovering in the event of an unforeseen set of circumstances arising, such as just described. On the other hand, it is necessary to contain the herds to a size which is of manageable proportion in relation to the available facilities and resources. The third factor is that of visitor convenience: the deer should be numerous enough for them to be readily seen by the visitor. Although the park could safely carry more deer, it is considered that herds of about four hundred fallow and three hundred red satisfy those requirements.

There was one serious disadvantage in the supplementary winter feeding method employed after the abandonment of silage feeding. The method involved shovelling out the 'rations', once a day, from a moving tractor and trailer, following a long line in two open sites regularly used for the practice. Although something of a spectacle, particularly as the deer quickly learned to respond to the call of the 'feed' man, it was the strongest and heaviest animals which won the lion's share, at the expense of the weak, the small and the young.

In the late 1970s another difficulty was manifesting itself, in that the best pasture lands, basically the 140 hectares of parkland which had been under the plough during the war years, were losing their vigour, no doubt as a result of almost three decades of constant grazing by deer and sheep (four hundred ewes, with their lambs, were pastured each year from April to September) and the effects of trampling by many visitors. So in 1980 new management tactics were introduced. Partly to protect the grazing and partly because it is now accepted that grazing park deer and sheep on the same land can create a parasite problem debilitating to the deer, the practice of grazing sheep was discontinued. It is interesting to note that there is no record of sheep ever having been grazed in the open parkland prior to the Second World War, although cattle and horses were.

At the same time a pasture husbandry programme, involving the controlled use of a treated sewage sludge, was introduced in order to restore the vigour of the good pasture lands. The material is applied to selected areas in spring and is rapidly absorbed into the sward, although it releases plant nutrients evenly over a period of months. Aided by a single grass-cutting operation in summer, to maintain the vegetative growth of the sward at the expense of flowering, good grass growth is maintained until late in the year, and early, steady growth the following spring encouraged. This almost continuous growth of new grass has virtually eliminated the necessity of providing supplementary winter feed, apart from some hay in the hardest of winter weather, and the provision of nutrient mineral blocks during the winter. The treated sludge, supplied by Thames Water Authority, has been accepted as safe to use in a park to which the public have access; the sludge is carefully monitored through-out the lengthy preparation process, and the soil of the treated areas tested, before and after application. Over the past three years some eighty hectares of grassland have been treated, almost all of which were utilized for agriculture during the war.

Today Richmond Park caters for the enjoyment and recreation of a vast population. It attracts many visitors – not only from the many who live within easy reach but those who come from further afield and from overseas. The pressures placed upon it are ever increasing, and inevitably there is demand for change in response to those pressures. The presence of the motor vehicle has had perforce to be accepted. A limited proportion

Overleaf: A snow scene near the Isabella Plantation

of parkland has been sacrificed to the demands of modern sport, in the form of the two golf courses and the winter games pitches, although their impact has been successfully subdued by restricting them to a comparatively small specific location. An area of a thousand hectares in the midst of a huge urban conglomerate cannot avoid being drawn into the mechanisms of that conglomerate, and a number of public utility services – telecommunication cables, gas and water mains etc. – pass through the park, all of them underground and therefore not impinging upon the landscape. The essential associated maintenance services do, however, from time to time.

This heavy and varied use requires machinery to protect and control; hence the necessity of park regulations. Since it was first laid before Parliament in 1872, the Royal Parks and Gardens Regulations Act (Chapter 9) has been amended but twice – in 1926 and in 1974. Its purpose has not changed: not only is the intention to protect the parks and gardens which it embraces (those whose management is the responsibility of the Department of the Environment), but it also provides for the protection of all who make use of them. The Act has been amended only in response to a changing society. In order to emphasize that necessity, the 1974 amendment restored to the park-keeping force the status of a constabulary, and once again all park constables are required to be attested before a Justice of the Peace.

Despite all, Richmond Park has not yielded up its historic character. The park deer species of old thrive, without adulteration. The informal mixture of woodland, wasteland and 'lawns' survive and flourish, as do the Pen Ponds, still fishponds, reminiscent of the fishponds of a medieval park. The plantations, even that containing the Woodland Garden, would not be out of place in a medieval park. Richmond Park is a national monument of outstanding character, one which preserves the grand cycle of nature to the best advantage and is, at the same time, an active and important ingredient of modern society. It is fitting to return to the 1961 Report of the Ministry of Works Advisory Committee on Forestry for the final word. Richmond Park 'preserves a treasured example of the English landscape which, it is to be hoped, the public and the authorities will long continue in co-operation to protect and maintain'.

Left: An aerial view, 1980. Bog Lodge is in the centre, and the carriageway, described by James Sawyer as 'a very beautiful drive it is, having the appearance of a Royal Domain' (Chapter 7) is clearly visible

APPENDIX

The Police at Richmond Park from Punch *1872*

Facsimile from *Punch* vol. LXIII, 1872

Our Pedestrian Contributor on Sunday last week was stopped by a Policeman posted at the Sheen Gate of Richmond Park. The Policeman informed your Pedestrian Contributor, whose dog, *Crab*, accompanied him, that, by order, dogs were not to be admitted, unless led. This excellent regulation has always existed, and never been enforced within your Pedestrian Contributor's memory, and probably not within that of the oldest inhabitant. But, ha, ha! there are Policemen to enforce it now, placed on purpose.

Crab is a little dog, to be sure; no bigger than *Toby*. But, as the saying is, 'little dogs have long tails.' Besides, if little dogs were admitted into Richmond Park loose, great dogs would also have to be. It would be impossible to draw the line between little dogs and big. Some of the big dogs might sometimes attempt to run after the deer; and though most of them would be instantly called off, and would come, no doubt, a few might persist for perhaps two or even three minutes in chasing a few deer a few yards, and would thus seriously injure the deer, though indeed without biting them or frightening them quite to death.

The little dogs at the present season would, it is true, do no such great mischief to any of the game in Richmond Park as the large dogs might to the deer. Even in the breeding-months, when their masters were some-times invited by the Park Keepers to lead them, they never, to be sure, did worse than occasionally snap up a diminutive stray rabbit. But, neverthe-less, Sir, you know they would scratch the turf in places, and so deface it, although invisibly, and at spots extremely far apart. They might even do microscopical damage to the thistles and ferns; and though all the buttercups are now gone, they would possibly, here and there, ruffle a daisy.

Your Pedestrian Contributor, at the Policeman's bidding, summoned *Crab* to be secured. He takes a cord and collar out with *Crab* generally. *Crab*, being acquainted with his tether before, knew what was intended for him, and, being an animal as disobedient as sagacious, immediately ran ahead into the Park. The Policeman did not attempt to pursue *Crab*, and was graciously pleased not to arrest me, or prevent me from following him.

How happy, Sir, are we in living under a Government so extremely paternal that it now stations Policemen on the look-out for a purpose of comparatively so little, but positively of such immense, importance to the Public, as that of preventing dogs from frisking about for a few yards in Richmond Park! The mischief which has been done there by those animals is probably almost equal to that which poodles and bull-dogs, suffered to accompany their masters, do in the open and public parts of the New Forest. There are no deer at all now in the Forest; but there are very many more flowers growing there than all that are to be found anywhere, at any time of the year, in Richmond Park, which is not like Kensington Gardens.

We fail sufficiently to appreciate the blessing of that freedom which we have come to enjoy in having a Policeman awaiting us at each step, to direct or check our proceedings and regulate our conduct, and we are not as yet duly awake to the delightful prospect of very soon being placed under Police supervision as much as ticket-of-leave-men, kept in order equally with the dangerous classes, and controlled by the Constabulary in every act of our lives.

References and Notes

For publishers, dates of publication etc, see Bibliography.

Chapter 1

1   *Domesday England*, H. C. Darby
2   *The Domesday Geography of South East England*, H. C. Darby and Eila M. J. Cambell. Darby and Cambell suggest that Oakley was probably associated with Bernwood Forest and that the Watchingwell entry was a reference to the later royal forest of Parkhurst
3   *Domesday Geography. Midland England*, H. C. Darby and L. B. Terret
4   'Sawyer Family Papers' (unpublished). An account of expenses submitted by James Sawyer in February 1798 for the cost of work carried out on the direction of the King
5   *The Royal Forests of Medieval England*, Charles R. Young, p. 4
6   *A General Introduction to Domesday Book*, Volume I, Sir Henry Ellis. Sir Henry Ellis quoted Canute's law in Latin, and I am indebted to Ronald Hase BA for kindly providing the translation
7   *Oxfordshire Parks*, Frank Woodward, p. 4
8   'The Medieval Parks of England', L. M. Cantor and J. Hatherlie, in *Geography*
9   *The History of the Kings Works*, Volume II, (ed.) H. M. Colvin
10   *Twicknam Parke*, Alan C. B. Urwin
11   *History of the Rebellion*, Book I, Edward Hyde, Earl of Clarendon, ed. W. Dunn Macray
12   *Fallow Deer*, Donald and Norma Chapman, p. 184
13   *Richmond Park. Extracts From the Records of Parliament and the Corporation of London*, Sir Thomas J. Nelson
14   PRO Reference Work 16–493. A letter, dated 11 June 1872, from the Lords Commissioners of HM Treasury to the Commissioner of Works
15   Richmond Park Traffic Survey 1973
16   'Trees in Richmond Park', HMSO, 1961

Chapter 2
1   *Fallow Deer*, Donald and Norma Chapman, Chapter 3
2   *A descriptive List of the Deer-Parks and Paddocks of England*, J. Whitaker
3   *Fallow Deer*, Donald and Norma Chapman, p. 26
4   Ibid., p. 147

Chapter 3
1   *The Royal Forests of Medieval England*, Charles R. Young, pp. 2–3
2   *A Treatise and Discourse of the Lawes of the Forest*, John Manwood, Charta de Foresta, cap. 11
3   Public Record Office, Ref. Work 16–788. *Note*: On file is a copy of a memorial prepared by Edward Tyrrell, Esq., Remembrancer of the City of London, and addressed to the Lords Commissioners of HM Treasury, dated August 1856. The Memorial traces the history of the Royal Venison Warrant, in relation to its association with the City of London, from the twelfth century
4   *Hunting and Stalking Deer in Britain through the Ages*, G. Kenneth Whitehead, p. 218, and Corporation of London Record Office
5   The British Library, Department of Manuscripts, Cotton MS Vespasian FXIII, f. 87
6   Corporation of London Record Office, City Cash Account, 1632–3, f. 64
7   Calendar, State Papers, Domestic, James I, volume XXXIX, Item 73, 1608
8   Public Record Office, Ref. Work 16–493
9   Public Record Office, Ref. Work 6–127, 1–3, Royal Warrants
10 Public Record Office, Ref. Work 3–7
11 Ibid., Ref. Work 16–493
12 Ibid., Ref. Work 6–128, 39–43
13 Royal Archives, Royal Household Menus
14 Public Record Office, Ref. Work 6–129 and 130
15 Ibid., Ref. Work 16–547. Correspondence between Sir Lionel Earl, Office of Works, and Sir Derek Keppel, Master of the Household, Buckingham Palace
16 Ibid.
17 Ibid., Ref. Work 16–546 and 554
18 Ibid., Ref. Work 16–1711
19 College of St George, Windsor Castle. Annual Audit Books – series beginning 1751–2
20 *The Royal Forests of Medieval England*, Charles R. Young, p. 115
21 *The History and Antiquities of Richmond, Petersham and Ham*, E. Beresford Chancellor, p. 42
22 Corporation of London Record Office, Repertories of the Court of Alderman for the Corporation, various references
23 Public Record Office, Ref. Work 16–495, Sign Manuals of George III dated 8 December 1780 and 1 April 1782
24 Royal Archives, PP Household, Vol. 11/1043

Chapter 4

1 'The Growth of Richmond', John Cloake, Richmond Society, History Section
2 Calendars of Patent Rolls, 1436–41, p. 416
3 *Some Account of English Deer Parks*, E. P. Shirley. Shirley gives as his source *Letters of Queen Margaret of Anjou* printed by the Camden Society in 1863
4 *The History and Antiquities of Richmond, Kew, Petersham and Ham*, E. Beresford Chancellor, Appendix B. Chancellor states that the extract is from an old work, reprinted in the *Antiquarian Repertory*
5 Ibid., p. 42
6 *History and Antiquities of the County of Surrey*, Manning and Bray, Volume III, p. 306, 1814, and Public Record Office, Ref. C214/884
7 Calendars of State Papers, Domestic, Charles I, 1629–31, Volume CLXXXL, 32, 1630 (?)
8 Public Record Office, Enclosure Map, Richmond New Park, Ref. LRRO 1/385, MR 295
9 Public Record Office, Ref. LRRO 1/576, MR 675. 'An Exact Survey of the Citys of London, Westminster, Borough of Southwark and the Country Near Ten Miles Around. Begun in 1741 and ended in 1745,' John Rocque, engraved by Richard Parr
10 Calendar, Treasury Books, Volume III, part ii, 1669–72, p. 782 (Early XVA pp. 107, 139–40, 8 Feb. 1671)
11 *History of the Rebellion*, Edward Hyde, Earl of Clarendon, ed. W. Dunn Macray
12 *History and Antiquities of the County of Surrey*, Manning and Bray, Volume I, p. 415
13 *Monarchy and the Chase*, 'Sabretache', p. 83. *Note*: The author quotes from *Prince Rupert and the Cavaliers* by Eliot Warburton, published in 1849
14 Ordnance Survey sheet 'Royal Parks. Richmond Park', Director General of the Ordnance Survey, Southampton (Park revised 1968)
15 Public Record Office, Ref. LRRO 1/375 MPE 426. 'A Plan of His Majesty's New Park at Richmond Surrey', John Eyre, 1754
16 Calendar, Treasury Books, Volume XIV, 1698–9, p. 154
17 *Gleanings in Natural History*, Edward Jesse, 1st Ed. Volume I, p. 159 and Volume III, p. 244
18 Calendar, State Papers, Domestic, Charles I, 1637, Volume CCLXIV, 92, 30 July 1637
19 Ibid., Volume CCCLXIII, 38, 6 July 1637
20 Public Record Office, Ref. Work 5–176/4
21 *Richmond Park. Extracts from the Records of Parliament and the Corporation of London*, Sir Thomas J. Nelson
22 *The Royal Forests of Medieval England*, Charles R. Young, pp. 163–4
23 Private correspondence with Professor G. W. S. Barrow, Dept of Scottish History, University of Edinburgh
24 *The Correspondence of Bishop Brian Duppa and Sir Justinian Isham 1650–60*, ed. Sir Gyles Isham, footnotes to pp. 33–4
25 *The Burlington Magazine*, Volume XCVI, no. 618, pp. 275–7

26 Calendar, State Papers, Domestic, Charles I, 1636–7, Volume CCXLVIII, I, 23 February 1637
27 Ibid., Volume CCCXXXIX, 15, 1636 (?)
28 *History of the Royal Buckhounds*, J. P. Hore, p. 143
29 *A History of Richmond Park*, C. L. Collenette, p. 147. *Note*. The author quotes from a letter written by Col Edmund Whalley
30 Corporation of London Record Office, City Cash Account 1652, Volume I/8, f. 53b and City Cash Account 1658, Volume II/9, f. 144b
31 Corporation of London Record Office, Repertories of the Court of Aldermen for the Corporation, Repertory 60, f. 66, f. 796–80, f. 135b, f. 181
32 Corporation of London Record Office, Repertories of the Court of Aldermen for the Corporation, Repertory 61, f. 122b, Repertory 63, f. 284b
33 Corporation of London Record Office, City Cash account 1652, Volume I/8, f. 54b
34 Corporation of London Record Office, Journal of the Common Council, Journal 41. f. 83b
35 Corporation of London Record Office, Repertories of the Court of Aldermen for the Corporation, Repertory 61. f. 218
36 Corporation of London Record Office, Repertories of the Court of Aldermen for the Corporation, Repertory 63, f. 204b
37 *A History of Richmond Park*, C. L. Collenette, pp. 10–11

Chapter 5
1 Calendar, State Papers, Domestic, Charles II, 1661–2, Volume LII, 35, 7 March 1662 (Ent. Book 5. p. 196. 7 March 1662)
2 *Correspondence of Bishop Brian Duppa and Sir Justinian Isham 1650–60* ed. Sir G. Isham
3 *Richmond Park. Portrait of a Royal Playground*, Pamela Fletcher Jones, p. 20
4 Calendar, State Papers, Domestic, Charles II, 1660–61, Volume VIII, July 1660 (Doquet Book, p. 19)
5 Calendar, State Papers, Domestic, Charles II, 1660–61, Volume XI, August 1660 (Doquet Book, p. 35)
6 Calendar, Treasury Books, Volume I, 1660–67, p. 424 (Early Entry Book 3, p. 437, 6 September 1662)
7 Calendar, State Papers, Domestic. Charles II, 1660–61, Volume XXII, 188, November (?) 1660
8 Calendar, State Papers, Domestic, Charles II, 1661–62, Volume XXXIX, 69, 19 July 1661 (Doquet)
9 Calendar, State Papers, Domestic, Charles II, 1663–4, Volume LXIX, 67, 13 March 1663 (Ent Book 9, pp. 326–7)
10 Calendar, State Papers, Domestic, Charles II, 1667–8, 28 December 1667 (Ent. Book 17, p. 274)
11 Calendar, State Papers, Domestic, Charles II, 1667–8, 18 August 1668
12 Calender, State Papers, Domestic, Charles II, 1667–8, 25 August and 27 August 1668

13 Calendar, State Papers, Domestic, Charles II, undated papers 1668, (SP Dom., Car. 11, 251, no. 144)

14 Calendar, Treasury Books. Volume III, part i, 1669–72, p. 178 (Treasury Minute Book III, pp. 3–5, 8 January 1669)

15 Ibid., p. 146

16 Ibid., p. 151

17 Calendar, Treasury Books, Volume III, part ii, 1669–72, p. 998 and p. 1161. *Note*: The Commission members are recorded as Sir Nicholas Carew, Sir C. Harbord, Sir Paul Neal, Sir William Haward, Sir John Talbot, Sir Thomas Clarges, Sir William Poultney, Henry Slingsby and William Harbord. The Commissioner's Articles of Introduction – to view the lodges etc. and the condition of the officers, what lodges they hold and by what title, supply of hay for the deer, timber felled, deer killed, sports, waste or destruction.

18 Calendar, State Papers, Domestic, Charles II, 1663–4, Volume LXXXV, 62, 10 December 1663

19 Calendar, State Papers, Domestic, Charles II, 1667–8, undated papers 1667 (SP Dom., Car. 11 230, no. 82)

20 Calendar, State Papers, Domestic, Charles II, 1664–5, Volume C11, 90, 20 September 1664 (Ent. Book 16, p. 239)

21 *Fallow Deer*, Donald and Norma Chapman, pp. 203–4

22 Calendar, Treasury Books, Volume II, 1667–8, p. 373 (Treasury Minute Book 11, pp. 239–41, 6 July 1668)

23 Ibid., p. 641. *Note*: There are further references to bricks being made on site on pp. 471, 502 and 505 of the same volume

24 Calendar, State Papers, Domestic, Charles II, 1673, Volume XV, 8 May 1673

25 *Tales of a Grandfather*, Sir Walter Scott, Chapter LI

26 Calendar, Treasury Books, Volume IV, 1672–5, p. 376 (Warrants Not Relating to Money III, pp. 475–6, 28 July 1673)

27 *A History of Richmond Park*, C. L. Collenette, p. 31 and Public Record Office, C5/85/96 and C5/97/43

28 Calendar, Treasury Books, Volume III, part ii, 1669–72, p. 782 (Early XVA, pp. 107, 139–40, 8 February 1671)

29 Calendar, State Papers, Domestic, Charles II, 1676–7, 17 November 1676 (Home Office Warrant Book 1. p. 226)

30 Calendar, Treasury Books, Volume VI, 1679–80, p. 550 (Out Letters, General, p. 512, 24 May 1680)

31 Ibid., p. 589 (Warrants Not Relating to Money, p. 195, 25 June 1680)

32 *Richmond Park. Portrait of a Royal Playground*, Pamela Fletcher Jones, p. 24

33 Calendar, Treasury Books, Volume VIII, part i, 1685–9, p. 3 (King's Warrant Book, p. 21, 17 February 1685)

34 Calendar, Treasury Books, Volume XIV, 1698–9, p. 154

35 Calendar, State Papers, Domestic, William and Mary, 1697, 30 November 1697

36 Calendar, State Papers, Domestic, William and Mary, 1698, 4 February 1698

37 *A History of Richmond Park*, C. L. Collenette, p. 15 (quoting *Rariora*, J. E. Hodgkin, Volume III, 1902)

38 *Hunting and Stalking Deer in Britain Through the Ages*, Kenneth G. Whitehead, p. 22. *Note*: It is claimed by some that the King's riding accident took place in Bushy Park, and not Richmond

39 *A Collection of Ordinances and Regulations for the Government of the Royal Household from King Edward III to King William and Queen Mary*, The Society of Antiquaries (from a MS in the Harleian Library, no. 5010)

40 Calendar, Treasury Books, Volume XIV, 1698–9, p. 259, 31 January 1699

41 Calendar, Treasury Books, Volume XXIX, part ii, 1714–15 (Order Book IX, p. 24, 9 December 1714) and Calendar, Treasury Books Volume XXVIII, part ii, 1714, p. 102

42 Calendar, Treasury Books. Volume XXX, part ii, 1716, p. 470 (Money Book XXIV, p. 551b, 18 September 1716)

43 Public Record Office, Ref. LRRO 1/375, MPE 426, 'A Plan of His Majesty's New Park at Richmond in Surrey', John Eyre, 1754

44 *History of the Royal Buckhounds*, J. P. Hore, p. 300. *Note*: Unfortunately the author gives no source for this

45 *A History of Richmond Park*, C. L. Collenette, p. 28

46 *Richmond Park. Portrait of a Royal Playground*, Pamela Fletcher Jones, p. 25

47 Calendar, Treasury Books, Volume CLIX, 1708–14, p. 471

48 Calendar, Treasury Books, Volume XXX, part ii, 1716, p. 281 (Ref. Book IX, p. 280, 14 June 1716)

49 *A History of Richmond Park*, C. L. Collenette, p. 14

50 *Memoirs of the Reign of King George the Second*, Horace Walpole

Chapter 6

1 *The Works of the Right Hon. Lady Mary Wortley Montagu*, ed. J. Dallaway, Volume III

2 *Bygone Richmond*, H. M. Cundall

3 *Letters to and from Henrietta, Countess of Suffolk, from 1712 to 1767*, ed. J. W. Croker

4 *Hunting and Stalking Deer in Britain Through the Ages*, Kenneth G. Whitehead, p. 31. *Note*: Whitehead adds that the stag responsible for this incident was spared, by command of the King, so that 'he might be hunted again'

5 *A History of Richmond Park*, C. L. Collenette, p. 148

6 *History of the Royal Buckhounds*, J. P. Hore, pp. 257–79. *Note*: The information is from tables showing the meets of the Royal Buckhounds between 1728 and 1739

7 Ibid., pp. 224–5

8 Ibid., pp. 306–7

9 Calendar, Treasury Books, 1735–8. (Treasury Minute Book XXVII, p. 402)

10 *A Tract on the National Interest, and Depravity of the Times in which the Subjects Claim to certain Rights in R. P. are fully considered and digested*, Published by J. Shepheard, London, 1757. The extension of the fence month is also

described in a second slim volume: *Two Historic Accounts of the Making of New Forest in Hampshire by King William the Conqueror; and Richmond New Park by King Charles the First*, published by M. Cooper, London, 1751

11 *A History of Richmond Park*, C. L. Collenette, p. 17
12 Ibid., pp. 46–7 and *History of the King's Works*, general editor H. M. Colvin, p. 230
13 Calendar, Treasury Books, Volume I, 1729–30 p. 72 (Treasury Minute Book XXVI, pp. 209–10, 20 May 1729) and Ibid., p. 82 (Lord Chamberlain's Warrant Book I, p. 300)
14 Calendar, Treasury Books, Volume III, 1735–6, p. 256
15 *A History of Richmond Park*, C. L. Collenette, p. 40
16 Public Record Office, Ref. LRRO, 1/576, MR 675
17 Public Record Office, Ref. LRRO 1/375, MPE 426
18 *History of the Royal Buckhounds*, J. P. Hore, p. 299
19 Calendar, Treasury Books, Volume II, 1731–4, p. 387
20 Calendar, Treasury Books, Volume I, 1735–8, p. 222, 18 June 1736
21 Calendar, Treasury Books, Volume V, 1742–5, p. 114 (Warrants not relating to money, XXVII pp. 14–15)
22 *History of the Royal Buckhounds*, J. P. Hore, p. 239
23 Calendar, Treasury Books, Volume V, 1742–5, p. 183 (Money Book XLI pp. 42–3)
24 *History of the Royal Buckhounds*, J. P. Hore, p. 321
25 *A History of Richmond New Park*, by 'A Resident'. *Note*: A manuscript note in the Richmond Library copy of this book suggests that the 'resident' was John Lucas, a member of the Lucas family associated with the park in the eighteenth and nineteenth centuries
26 Calendar, Treasury Books Volume II, 1731–41, p. 215 (Treasury Minute Book XXXII, p. 98, February 1732)
27 Calendar, Treasury Books Volume III, 1735–8, p. 411. (Money Book XXXVIII, p. 500, April 1734)
28 Calendar, Treasury Books Volume V, 1742–5, p. 406 (Money Book XLI, p. 236, 21 June 1743)
29 *Fallow Deer*, D. and N. Chapman, p. 184
30 *A History of Richmond Park*, C. L. Collenette, p. 44
31 Ibid., pp. 19–20 and *Richmond Park. Portrait of a Royal Playground*, P. Fletcher Jones, pp. 29–31
32 Calendar, Home Office Papers, George II, 1760–65, 25 June 1761
33 *History of the Royal Buckhounds*, J. P. Hore, p. 373
34 *A History of Richmond Park*, C. L. Collenette, p. 67
35 *History of the Royal Buckhounds*, J. P. Hore, p. 195
36 *Gleanings in Natural History*, Edward Jesse, Volume I, pp. 136–7, 4th ed
37 Public Record Office, Ref. Work 16–407. Correspondence between the Hon. James Stuart and the Lords Commissioners of HM Treasury, March 1789
38 Sawyer Family Papers (unpublished)
39 Public Record Office, Ref. Work 16–35/1
40 *A History of Richmond New Park*, by 'A Resident', p. 60

Chapter 7

1 *A History of Richmond Park*, C. L. Collenette, pp. 20–21
2 Trees in Richmond Park, HMSO, 1961
3 Sawyer Family Papers. Handwritten unpublished autobiography by James Sawyer entitled 'Narrative of a Yeoman'
4 *A History of Richmond Park*, C. L. Collenette, p. 21. *Note*: Collenette gives as his source the *General View of the Agriculture of Surrey* by W. James and J. Malcolm, published in 1794
5 *Richmond Park. Portrait of a Royal Playground*, P. Fletcher Jones, pp. 40–41, and *The History and Antiquities of Richmond*, E. Beresford Chancellor, p. 228
6 *Richmond Park. Portrait of a Royal Playground*, P. Fletcher Jones, pp. 32–3
7 Public Record Office. Ref. Work 6–294, letters from and to Office of Woods etc.
8 Public Record Office. Ref. Work 5–210, Accounts
9 'Plan of His Majesty's Park Call'd Richmond New Park in the County of Surrey', Thos. Richardson, 1771, Public Record Office, Ref. LRRO 1/386, MR 296
10 *A History of Richmond New Park*, by 'A Resident', p. 37
11 Sawyer Family Papers: Sawyer 'family tree'
12 Sawyer Family Papers. 'An Account of Expenses in November 1797 and February 1798'
13 *Gleanings in Natural History*, Edward Jesse, 4th ed., II, p. 338
14 Ibid., pp. 338–9
15 *A History of Richmond Park*, C. L. Collenette, p. 28
16 Sawyer Family Papers. 'Narrative of a Yeoman'
17 *The English Garden*, Ralph Dutton
18 Public Record Office, Ref. Work 3–46
19 Public Record Office, 'Plan of the Crown's Richmond Park Estate and Sudbrook Park in the County of Surrey', 1850, Ref. Work 16–3/2
20 *Gleanings in Natural History*, Edward Jesse, 1st ed., Volume I, p. 156
21 Ibid., Volume III, p. 245
22 *A History of Richmond Park*, C. L. Collenette, pp. 54–5
23 Public Record Office, Ref. Work 16–4/5
24 *A History of Richmond Park*, C. L. Collentte, p. 55
25 Public Record Office, Ref. Work 3–7
26 *A History of Richmond New Park*, by 'A Resident', p. 38
27 Sawyer Family Papers. Diaries of James Sawyer, Head Keeper, Richmond Park, 1825–70
28 Ibid., James Sawyer, a receipt from his servant Wm. Bishop for a year's wages: £12, 1789
29 *A History of Richmond Park*, C. L. Collenette, p. 66

Chapter 8

1 Sawyer Family Papers. Diaries of James Sawyer, Head Keeper, Richmond Park. 1825–70
2 *A History of Richmond Park*, C. L. Collenette, pp. 54–5, and Sawyer Family Papers

3   Sawyer Family Papers: Sawyer 'family tree'
4   *Gleanings in Natural History*, Edward Jesse, 4th ed., Volume II, pp. 339–40
5   Public Record Office, Ref. Work 16–407, various reports and correspondence
6   *Deer and Their Management in the Deer Parks of Great Britain and Ireland*, Kenneth G. Whitehead
7   Public Record Office, Ref. Work 3–8, Ledger of Office of Woods letters 1839–51
8   Public Record Office, Ref. LRRO 1/375, MPE 426, 1754 Plan of Richmond Park
9   Ibid., Ref. 16–3/2, 1850 Plan of Richmond Park
10 Public Record Office, Ref. Work 3–46
11 Public Record Office, Ref. Work 16–407 (Report on the Costs of Maintaining the Royal Parks Deer Herds), 1848, and Ref. Work 3–46
12 'Master of the Horses' Department', the Royal Mews, Buckingham Palace
13 Sawyer Family Papers. Diaries of James Sawyer, Head Keeper, Richmond Park, 1825–70, entry for 27 October 1835 – 'Sent the boys to get chestnuts in the Spankers Hill plantation'
14 *A History of Richmond New Park*, by 'A Resident', p. 45
15 Sawyer Family Papers. Diaries of James Sawyer, Head Keeper, Richmond Park, 1825–70
16 Ibid.
17 Ibid.
18 Sawyer Family Papers. Various references, including Henry Sawyer's instructions for the use of his newly invented breach gun
19 *The Book of the Gun*, Harold L. Peterson, pp. 160–85
20 The Armouries, HM Tower of London. Private correspondence with Mr G. M. Wilson, Deputy Master of the Armouries, 1981
21 *Monarchs of the Glen*, Duff Hart Davis, p. 83
22 *A History of Richmond New Park*, by 'A Resident', p. 45

Chapter 9
1   Public Record Office, Ref. Work 16–239
2   Sawyer Family Papers. Diaries of James Sawyer, Head Keeper, Richmond Park, 1825–70
3   Public Record Office, Ref. Work 16–4/1
4   Sawyer Family Papers. Diaries of James Sawyer, Head Keeper, Richmond Park, 1825–70
5   Ibid., 'A letter to Mr. Sawyer, His Majesty's Park Keeper, Richmond Park, Surrey from Mr. J. R. I. Turner at His Majesty's Command. Dated November 27, 1825'
6   Ibid., Diaries of James Sawyer, Head Keeper, Richmond Park, 1825–70
7   Public Record Office, Ref. Work 16–215
7a 'The Manor of Coombe', Occasional Paper No. 3, Kingston-on-Thames Archaeological Society, 1979
8   *History of Richmond Park*, C. L. Collenette, p. 48

9   Ibid., pp. 51–2
10 Public Record Office, Ref. Work 3–46. Letter addressed to James Sawyer, Head Keeper, Richmond Park, from Lord John Russell, 23 April 1856
11 Sawyer Family Papers. Diaries of James Sawyer, Head Keeper, Richmond Park, 1825–70
12 *History of Richmond Park*, C. L. Collenette, p. 23
13 Public Record Office, Ref. Work 16–407
14 *Gleanings in Natural History*, Edward Jesse, 4th ed., Volume II, p. 339
15 *Red Deer Stalking in New Zealand*, T. E. Donne
16 *Origin, Release and Potential of the Rakaia Red Deer Herd*, D. B. Banwell
17 *A Descriptive List of the Deer Parks and Paddocks of England*, Joseph Whitaker, p. 23
18 'The History of the Introduction of Deer to Otago', P. Harker (Otago Acclimatisation Society)
19 *A History of Richmond Park*, C. L. Collenette, p. 24, and large-scale Office of Works plans of Richmond Park dated 1856 and 1864
20 *A History of Richmond New Park*, by 'A Resident', p. 47. *Note*: Extracts of Annual Expenditure on Richmond Park taken from the Royal Park and Public Gardens Books
21 Richmond Park, Department of the Park Bailiff, Cash Account Book 1868–77
22 Public Record Office, Ref. Work 16–493
23 Ibid., Treasury letter to the First Commissioner of Works, 11 June 1872
24 *A History of Richmond New Park*, by 'A Resident', pp. 45–6
25 Public Record Office, Ref. Work 16–215, a draft Warrant of appointment, 1857
26 *A History of Richmond Park*, C. L. Collenette, pp. 29–30
27 Ibid., p. 32
28 *A History of Richmond New Park*, by 'A Resident', p. 44
29 'Trees in Richmond Park', HMSO, 1961
30. Richmond Park, Department of the Park Bailiff, Cash Account Book 1868–77, entries for Jan., Mar., Dec. 1875
31 Ibid.

Chapter 10
1   *Fallow Deer*, Donald and Norma Chapman, p. 206
2   'Report on the Outbreak of Rabies among Deer in Richmond Park during the Years 1886–87', A. C. Cope, HMSO
3   Sawyer Family Papers. A letter from Henry Sawyer of Petworth Park to James Sawyer of Richmond Park, 25 February 1798
4   Ibid., 18 January 1795
5   Public Record Office. Ref. Work 16–407
6   *London's Natural History*, R. S. R. Fitter, p. 180
7   *Fallow Deer*, Donald and Norma Chapman, p. 148
8   *A Descriptive List of The Deer-Parks and Paddocks of England*, Joseph Whitaker, p. 11
9   Public Record Office, Ref. Work 16–493

10 *Wild England of Today*, C. J. Cornish, pp. 120–123. *Note*: The author claims that the 'catch-up' involved only largest stags, which were removed to Windsor Park 'in case they should prove a source of danger to the public in the rutting season'. The rutting season is confined, by and large, to late September and October, and thus long past by January. A more feasible destination for the 'catch-up' of stags witnessed by Cornish was the Royal Hunt paddock

11 Ibid., p. 125

12 'Trees in Richmond Park', HMSO, 1961

13 *Edward VII – A Portrait*, Christopher Hibbert, pp. 21–2

14 Public Record Office. Ref. Work 16-4-1

15 *A History of Richmond Park*, C. L. Collenette, p. 25

16 Public Record Office, Ref. Work 16-4-1 and Work 16-215

17 Richmond Park, Department of the Park Bailiff, Cash Account Book 1868–77

18 Public Record Office, Ref. Work 16–408, Report on the Deer Herds of Richmond Park dated 30 April 1907

19 Public Record Office. Ref. Work 812, a letter, dated 25 October 1904, from S. Pullman, Superintendent, Richmond Park, to Major Hussey, Bailiff of the Royal Parks

20 Public Record Office, Ref. Work 16–408, a letter, dated 2 July 1909, from the Board of Green Cloth to the Secretary, HM Office of Works

21 Ibid., a minute, dated August 1908, from the First Commissioner of Works to the Master of the Royal Household

Chapter 11

1   Public Record Office. Ref. Work 16–407, Richmond Park, Annual Report on Deer, April 1906

2   Public Record Office. Ref. Work 16–408, Richmond Park, Annual Deer Reports, 1906–15

3   Public Record Office, Ref. Work 16–1062

4   *Hunting and Stalking Deer in Britain through the Ages*, G. Kenneth Whitehead, pp. 208, 227, 242

5   Public Record Office, Ref. Work 3–47

6   *Hunting and Stalking Deer in Britain through the Ages*, G. Kenneth Whitehead, p. 243

7   Public Record Office, Ref. Work 16–408, Richmond Park, Annual Deer Report, April 1909

8   *The Handbook of Richmond Park*, Coryn de Vere

9   Public Record Office. Ref. Work 16–408, Richmond Park, Annual Deer Report. April 1910

10 Ibid., April 1912

11 *A History of Richmond Park*, C. L. Collenette, p. 40

12 'Trees in Richmond Park', HMSO, 1961

13 Corporation of London, Record Office, City Cash Account

14 *A History of Richmond Park*, C. L. Collenette, p. 25, and Plan of Richmond Park dated 1915

15 Public Record Office, Ref. Work 3–47, Hand-written Ledger of Instructions, Notes etc.
16 Public Record Office, Ref. Work 16–1061, Richmond Park, Annual Report on Deer, April 1916
17 Public Record Office. Ref. Work 16–547, Correspondence between Sir Lionel Earle, Commissioner of Works, and Sir Derek Keppal, Master of the Royal Household, May 1918
18 Ibid., Ref. Work 16–1689, Memorandum from Park Superintendent, 2 Feb. 1922
19 Ibid., Richmond Park, Annual Report on Deer, May 1922
20 Ibid., a letter from Sir Lionel Earle to the owners of various deer parks dated 23 October 1922
21 Ibid., Correspondence between the Duke of Buccleugh and Sir Lionel Earle, 1923–4
22 *Border Highways and Lothian Lore*, T. Ratcliffe Barnett
23 Public Record Office, Ref. Work 16–1062, Richmond Park, Annual Report on Deer, May 1928
24 Ibid., May 1939
25 Robert Burns, 'To a Mouse'
26 Personal correspondence with the Hon. F. David Astor
27 *Hunting and Stalking Deer in Britain through the Ages*, G. Kenneth Whitehead, p. 244
28 Plan of Richmond Park dated 1915
29 Public Record Office, Ref. Work 16–1689
30 Ibid., Ref. Work 16–1430
31 Ibid., Ref. Work 16–1122

Chapter 12
1 Ordnance Survey Sheet 'Royal Parks. Richmond Park', Director General of the Ordnance Survey, Chessington, Surrey, 1949
2 'Trees in Richmond Park', HMSO, 1961
3 Public Record Office, Ref. Work 16–1596, various reports and memoranda
4 *The Sunday Times*, 23 February 1941
5 Public Record Office, Ref. Work 16–1519
6 Ibid., Ref. Work 16–1596
7 *The Daily Telegraph*, 17 January 1950
8 *The Surrey Comet*, 11 February 1956
9 Public Record Office, Ref. Work 16–1895
10 'Trees in Richmond Park', HMSO, 1961
11 Public Record Office, Ref. LRRO, 1/386, MR 296
12 *Isabella Plantation*, Leaflet Guide, text Michael B. Brown, HMSO, 1980
13 *A History of Richmond Park*, C. L. Collenette, p. 64
14 *Gleanings in Natural History*, Edward Jesse, 4th ed., Volume II, pp. 208–9
15 *A History of Richmond Park*, C. L. Collenette, pp. 138–9
16 Personal correspondence with Dr P. M. Hammond, Principal Scientific Officer, British Museum (Natural History)

17 *Bird Life in the Royal Parks 1976*, A Report by the Committee on Bird Sanctuaries in the Royal Parks, Department of the Environment, London, January 1978

18 *A History of Richmond Park*, C. L. Collenette, p. 74

19 *Gleanings in Natural History*, Edward Jesse, 4th ed., Volume II, pp. 287 and 291

20 *London's Natural History*, R. S. R. Fitter, pp. 214–15

21 *A History of Richmond New Park*, by 'A Resident', p. 45

22 *Gleanings in Natural History*, Edward Jesse, 4th ed., Volume II, p. 20

23 *A History of Richmond Park*, C. L. Collenette, p. 138

24 *The Evening News*, 13 January 1958, '50 Years Ago' feature

Bibliography

BOOKS

Anon., *A Tract on the National Interest, and Depravity of the Times in which the Subjects Claim to certain Rights in R P are fully considered and digested.* (J. Sheppeard, London, 1757)

Anon., *Two Historic Accounts of the Making of New Forest in Hampshire by King William the Conqueror; and Richmond New Park by King Charles the First* (published for M. Cooper, London, 1751)

Barnett, T. R., *Border By-ways and Lothian Lore* (John Grant Booksellers Ltd, Edinburgh, 1943)

Chancellor, E. B., *The History and Antiquities of Richmond, Petersham and Ham* (Hiscoke & Son, Richmond, 1894)

Chapman, D. and N., *Fallow Deer* (Terence Dalton Ltd, Suffolk, 1975)

Collenette, C. L., *A History of Richmond Park* (Sidgwick & Jackson Ltd, London, 1937)

Colvin, H. M. (General Editor), *The History of the King's Works*, 6 vols. (HMSO, 1963–73)

Cornish, C. J., *Wild England of Today* (Seeley & Co., London, 1895)

Croker, J. W. (Editor), *Letters to and from Henrietta, Countess of Suffolk from 1712 to 1767* (John Murray, London, 1824)

Cundell, H. M., *Bygone Richmond* (John Lane, Bodley Head, 1925)

Dallaway, J. (Editor), *The Works of the Right Hon. Lady Mary Wortley Montague*, 5 vols. (Richard Phillips, London, 1803)

Darby, H. C., *Domesday England* (Cambridge University Press, 1977)

Darby, H. C. and Cambell, E. M. J., *The Domesday Geography of South East England* (Cambridge University Press, 1962)

Darby, H. C. and Terrett L. B., *Domesday Geography. Midland England*, 2nd. ed. (Cambridge University Press, 1971)

Davis, D. H., *Monarchs of the Glen* (Jonathan Cape, London, 1978)

Donne, T. E., *Red Deer Stalking in New Zealand* (Constable & Co. Ltd, London, 1924)

Dutton, R., *The English Garden*, 2nd ed. (B. T. Batsford Ltd, London, 1950)

Ellis, Sir H., *A General Introduction to Domesday Book* (Genealogical Publishing Co. Inc., Baltimore, 1973)

Fitter, R. S. R., *London's Natural History* (Collins, London, 1945)

Gascoigne, B., *Images of Richmond* (St Helena Press, 1978)

Hibbert, C., *Edward VII – A Portrait* (Penguin Books Ltd, 1982)

Hore, J. P., *History of the Royal Buckhounds* (Remington & Co. Ltd, London, 1893)

Hyde, Edward, Earl of Clarendon, *History of the Rebellion*, Book I, W. Dunn Macray, Editor (Clarendon Press, London, 1888)

Isham, Sir G., (Editor), *The Correspondence of Bishop Brian Duppa and Sir Justinian Isham, 1650–60* (The Northampton Record Society, Lamport Hall, Northants, 1955)

Jesse, E., *Gleanings in Natural History*, 2 vols., 4th ed. (John Murray, London, 1838)

Jones, P. F., *Richmond Park. Portrait of a Royal Playground* (Phillimore, London and Chichester, 1972)

Manning, Rev. O. and Bray, W., *History and Topography of the County of Surrey* British Library edition, 30 vols. (1847)

Manwood, J., *A Treatise and Discource of the Laws of the Forest* (Thomas Wight and Bonham, 1598)

Nelson, Sir T. J., *Richmond Park. Extracts from the Records of Parliament and the Corporation of London* (Blades, East and Blades, London, 1883)

Peterson, H. L., *The Book of the Gun* (Hamlyn, London, 1963)

'A Resident', *A History of Richmond New Park* (W. H. and A. Nutting, London, 1877). *Note*: A Manuscript note in the Richmond Library copy of this book suggests that the author was John Lucas

'Sabretache', *Monarchy and the Chase* (Eyre & Spottiswoode, London, 1948)

Scott, Sir W., *Tales of a Grandfather* (Adam and Charles Black, London, 1893)

Shirley, E. P., *Some Account of English Deer Parks* (John Murray, London, 1867)

Society of Antiquaries, *A Collection of Ordinances and Regulations for the Government of the Royal Household from King Edward III to King William and Queen Mary*

Urwin, A. C. B., *Twicknam Park* (published by the author, 1965)

Vere, Coryn de, *The Handbook of Richmond Park* (Knapp, Drewet & Sons Ltd, London, 1909)

Walpole, H., *Memoirs of the Reign of King George the Second*, 3 Vols. (Henry Colburn, London, 1846)

Whitaker, J., *A Descriptive List of the Deer-Parks and Paddocks of England* (Ballantyne, Hanson & Co., London, 1892)

Whitehead, G. K., *Deer and Their Management in the Deer Parks of Great Britain and Ireland* (Country Life Ltd., London 1950)

Whitehead, G. K., *Hunting and Stalking Deer in Britain through the Ages* (B. T. Batsford Ltd, London, 1980)

Woodward, F., *Oxfordshire Parks* (Oxford Museum Services, 1982)

Young, C. R., *The Royal Forests of Medieval England* (University of Pennsylvania Press, 1979)

Published Articles, Papers, Reports

Banwell, D. B., 'Origin, Release and Potential of the Rakaia Red Deer Herd', New Zealand, 1980

Cantor, L. M. and Hatherlie, J., 'The Medieval Parks of England', *Geography*, Volume LXIV, part ii, pp. 71–85, April 1979

Cloake, J., 'The Growth of Richmond', The Richmond Society, History Section, Paper No. 1, 1982

Gent, L. E., 'The Manor of Coombe and Coombe Nevill in Kingston upon Thames', Kingston upon Thames Archaeological Society, Occasional Paper No. 3, 1979

Harker, P., 'The History of the Introduction of Deer to Otago', Otago Acclimatisation Society, Dunedin, New Zealand, 1973

HMSO, 'Isabella Plantation. Woodland Garden, Richmond Park', text by Michael B. Brown, 1980

HMSO, Reports by the Committee on Bird Sanctuaries in the Royal Parks

HMSO 'Report on the Outbreak of Rabies Among Deer in Richmond Park during the Years 1886–87', A. C. Cope, Chief Inspector, Agricultural Dept Privy Council Office, and Professor Victor Horsely BS, FRS etc., 1888

HMSO, 'Trees in Richmond Park', 5th Report of the Advisory Committee on Forestry (Royal Parks) for the Ministry of Works, 1961

London Borough of Richmond on Thames, 'Richmond Park Traffic Survey 1973'

Patten, J., 'How the Deer Parks Began. The Chase and the English Landscape', *Country Life*, 16 September 1971

Tonybee, Margaret and Isham, Eyles, 'Joan Carlile (1606–1679) – An Identification', *The Burlington Magazine*, Volume XCVI, No. 618, September 1954

Unpublished Sources

The Sawyer Family Papers. A collection of diaries, letters and notes relating to the Sawyer family. Mainly nineteenth century

Private correspondence – the author and the Hon. F. David Astor

Ibid. – the author and Professor G. W. S. Barrow, Dept of Scottish History, University of Edinburgh

Ibid. – the author and Dr P. Hammond, Principal Scientific Officer, British Museum (Natural History)

Ibid. – the author and G. M. Wilson, Deputy Master of the Armouries, HM Tower of London

Archives

CALENDARS
Calendar of Home Office Papers, George II
Calendar of Patent Rolls, 1436–41
Calendar of State Papers Domestic, James I

Calendar of State Papers Domestic, Charles I
Ibid., Charles II
Ibid., William and Mary
Calendars of Treasury Books and Papers, 1660–1743

CITY OF LONDON RECORDS OFFICE
City Cash Accounts
Journal of the Common Council
Repertories of the Court of Aldermen for the Corporation

COLLEGE OF ST GEORGE, WINDSOR CASTLE
Annual Audit Books – series beginning 1751–2

PUBLIC RECORDS OFFICE
Records of the Office of Works and the Ministry of Public Buildings and Works.
   Series:
Work 3 – Miscellaneous letter books
Work 5 – Accounts
Work 6 – Miscellaneous (Royal Gardens)
Work 16 – Royal Parks and Pleasure Gardens

RICHMOND PARK
Department of the Park Bailiff, Cash Account Book 1868–77

ROYAL ARCHIVES, WINDSOR CASTLE
PP Household, Vol. 11/1043
Royal Household Menus

SURREY RECORDS OFFICE
Ref. 266/14/1/2

Index